MISS JEKYLL

*Portrait of a Great
Gardener*

MISS JEKYLL

Portrait of a Great Gardener

by

BETTY MASSINGHAM

'Strength may wield the pond'rous spade,
May turn the clod, and wheel the compost home,
But elegance, chief grace the garden shows
And most attractive, is the fair result
Of thought, the creature of a polish'd mind.'

The Task, by William Cowper.

DAVID & CHARLES : NEWTON ABBOT

o 7153 5757 3

First published in 1966 by
Country Life Limited

© Betty Massingham 1966, 1973

*Printed in Great Britain
by Biddles Ltd Guildford Surrey
for David & Charles (Holdings) Limited
South Devon House Newton Abbot Devon*

TO THE MEMORY OF
'PIDGE' AND CHRISTOPHER

FRANCIS PETER KAY COOPER
(*27th September, 1953—1st December, 1962*)

CHARLES CHRISTOPHER CORNISH
(*24th November, 1939—1st February, 1965*)

Contents

9

Illustrations

ILLUSTRATIONS IN THE TEXT

Acknowledgments

I have to make many acknowledgments.

In the first place I must thank Mrs Robin Barber (great-great niece of Hercules Brabazon) for her generous help in producing folios, letters and paintings and for permission to reproduce any that I wished to select; Mr Christopher Hussey for his encouragement in the early days of the synopsis and for permission to quote often and at length from his biography of Sir Edwin Lutyens; Mr Harold Raymond for reading the script through many times in different stages and for his corrections, suggestions, and untiring readiness to help—but above all for his kindly wit.

I must mention also the time spared to me so willingly by the late Lady Emily Lutyens and the fact that she particularly asked me to state her husband's appreciation of all that Miss Jekyll had done for him. The late Mr Harold Falkner, F.R.I.B.A., was equally helpful with his memories of visits to Munstead Wood, giving valuable details, writing to me frequently and allowing me to quote from his letters.

I am grateful to the following for their kindness in reading certain chapters of the script with a view to corrections: Mr Denys Haynes (Keeper, Department of Greek and Roman Antiquities, British Museum); Mr W. A. Thorpe; Professor A. F. Havighurst; Mr Norman Hadden, V.H.M.; Mr Ralph Arnold; Mr A. J. Huxley.

Among the many whom I must thank for permission to quote from books, articles or letters, for personal recollections of Miss Jekyll and for introductions to people who knew her, are: Mrs Barnes-Brand; Mrs Arthur Simon; Miss Musgrave; Mrs E. V. Clark; Mrs E. A. Ritchie; Mr Michael Haworth-Booth; Mr W. T. Stearn (British Museum, Natural History); Mr Peter Hunt; Mr Coulson (Keeper, Department of Prints and Drawings, British Museum); Mr G. F. Wingfield Digby (Keeper, Department of Textiles, Victoria and Albert Museum); Mrs H. J. Massingham; Mr Geoffrey Grigson; Mr Oliver Hill, F.R.I.B.A.; Miss Dilys Powell; Mr Clarke, late Parks Superintendent, Scarborough; Miss E. M. Dance, Curator, Guildford Museum; Mrs H. Raymond; Mr John Cornforth; Mr Allen S. Bell of the National Register of Archives; Mr Jack Dove, Hove Borough Librarian, and

Miss Green; Mr A. L. Bullion, Chief Fire Officer, County of Somerset; Mr Herbert Cowley; Mrs Peter Mason; Patience Gray; Miss Celia Bigham; Mrs W. H. Davies; The Countess of Rosse and The National Trust (Nymans); Mrs Nathaniel Lloyd (Great Dixter); Mrs V. Martens (Millmead); Colonel and Mrs S. D. H. Pollen (Deanery Garden); Mr and Mrs R. O. G. Gardner (Munstead Wood); Mr Miles Hadfield; The Secretary, Pestalozzi Village, Seddlescombe; The Chief Librarian, Kensington and Chelsea Public Libraries; and especially Mr E. M. Forster who gave me permission to quote from the life of his great-aunt, Marianne Thornton, and for most kindly allowing me to draw a parallel with Miss Jekyll from one stage of her life.

For innumerable kindnesses and encouragement I would like to thank many personal friends and members of my family and among these I must especially mention my aunt, Miss Gosselin; my brother-in-law Godfrey Massingham; Dr Alfred Burlingham; my brother, Geoffrey le Marchant Gosselin and the late Mother Verena, Superior of the Convent of All Saints, London Colney.

I owe, as any biographer of Miss Jekyll must owe, a debt to her nephew, the late Francis Jekyll, who made the first record of her life and work, which was published two years after her death.

The following have kindly given permission for the inclusion of some of the illustrations: the Directors of the British Museum (Plates 3, 7, 8, 9, 11, 15, 16); the Directors of the National Portrait Gallery (Plates 1, 2, 12, 13, 51, 52); the Directors of the Tate Gallery (Plate 40) and Miss Marguerite Steen (Plate 40). I am indebted, too, to the Chairman of the Royal Horticultural Society for permission to reproduce photographs from *Curtis's Botanical Magazine, Dedication and Portraits, 1828-1927* (Plates 32, 34, 36) and to the *R.H.S. Journal* (Plate 18); and to the following for the loan of photographs and permission to reproduce them: Mrs Robin Barber (Plate I); Mrs John Eden (Plate 33); The Countess of Rosse and The National Trust (Plate 53); The Mistress and Fellows of Girton College (Plate 17); Mr John Hadfield (*The Saturday Book*) (Plate 4); The Chief Librarian, Kensington and Chelsea Public Libraries (Plate 5); Mr N. J. Prockter (Plate 19); Mr J. Downward (Plate 55); Thames and Hudson (photographs by Edwin Smith, Plates VI, 58, 59); Mr A. J. Huxley (Plates IV, V); Mr and Mrs J. Wolley Dod (Plate 35); The Trustees of the Watts Gallery (Plate 14); Mr David McKenna and Longmans, Green and Co. (for illustrations from *Wood and Garden* and *Home and Garden*) and Country Life Ltd (for many of the photographs from Miss Jekyll's books).

Acknowledgments

I would also like to mention with gratitude the help given to me by the staff of the London Library, for their consideration and their liberality in the lending of a number of books over a period of years, and also by the staff of the Country Life Book Department for their courtesy and willing help, and especially to Miss Hazle Claremont.

Lastly, I wish to thank my son, Adam, for his patient and cheerful help, even when precious hours during the school holidays were taken up by locating Jekyll gardens, and especially for his careful drawings made at Lindisfarne to show the door fitments designed by Lutyens, similar to those in use at Munstead Wood.

Introduction

Dr Arthur Waley, referring to his book on the life and work of Yuan Mei (Allen and Unwin, 1957) writes:

'The account I have given of Yuan Mei consists so largely of quotations from his works, both in prose and verse, as almost to be an anthology. It is certainly far from being what is called "a critical biography". Still less is it a Life and Times. . . .'[1]

What Dr Waley wrote about his work applies equally, except for the reference to verse, to this book about Miss Jekyll. Her writings speak for themselves.

Now that she is known as a great gardener it may be as well to remember that she thought of herself as an amateur and addressed herself to amateurs. She was never dogmatic in her suggestions nor condescending in her ideas. She often refers, in her books, to the atmosphere of a garden rather than to the quantity of rare plants it may contain: 'For I hold that the best purpose of a garden is to give delight and to give refreshment of mind, to soothe, to refine, and to lift up the heart in a spirit of praise and thankfulness.'[2] Sir George Sitwell has written: 'In the ancient world it was ever the greatest of the emperors and the wisest of the philosophers that sought peace and rest in a garden. By the olive groves . . . of the Academia Plato discussed with his followers the supremacy of reason, the identity of truth and goodness.'[3] But a peaceful atmosphere is not dependent on a large or stately garden. 'It is just in the way it is done that lies the whole difference between commonplace gardening and gardening that may rightly claim to rank as a fine art. Given the same space of ground and the same material, they may either be fashioned into a dream of beauty, a place of perfect rest and refreshment of mind or body . . . or they may be so mis-used that everything is jarring and displeasing.'[4]

A big question must, I think, arise in one's mind. Are there any gardens left with her planting still intact? There are gardens which she designed, but it must be remembered that the changes of ownership

[1] *Times Literary Supplement.* 22nd February, 1957.
[2] Int. *Wood and Garden.* Gertrude Jekyll.
[3] *The Making of Gardens.* Sir George Sitwell.
[4] Int. *Colour Schemes for the Flower Garden.* Gertrude Jekyll.

over the years may make other changes, especially in that of atmosphere. As Sir William Temple wrote of his favourite garden: 'This was Moor Park when I was first acquainted with it, and the sweetest place, I think, that I have seen in my life; what it is now I can give little account, having passed through several hands that have made great changes in gardens as well as houses.'[1] Some of the best examples of her gardens are mentioned, and there must be others. Many of her ideas may be seen in gardens which are now open to the public—the R.H.S. Gardens, Wisley; the Savill Gardens, Windsor Great Park; Nymans, Sussex; Great Dixter, Northiam, Sussex; Sissinghurst Castle, Kent; Bodnant, Caernarvonshire—to mention only some of the bigger gardens, many of which are open daily.

But her ideas are in her books for all to read, and through her writing there emerges the kind of person that she was. This book is an attempt to give the story of her life and work, emphasising the development of her ideas from her training as an artist, through her study of Turner's paintings, the writings of Ruskin and William Morris, to her meeting with Lutyens and the manner in which she dealt with the problem of acute myopia. Her philosophy of life, her respect for humble plants, especially wild ones, as well as for Tibetan lilies or rare Himalayan poppies—these were all part of her character and personality.

'The wise will live by Faith,
Faith in the order of Nature and that her order is good'.[2]

Biddenden,
March, 1966

---

[1] Essay: *Upon the Gardens of Epicurus, or Of Gardening in the Year 1685*. Sir William Temple.
[2] *The Testament of Beauty*, Robert Bridges, 1st Oct. 1965, Oxford, 1929.

CHAPTER I

1843–1867

As a child—As a girl—As a young woman—
Journey to the Greek Islands

A preference for almond sweets coated with pink or white sugar and making daisy chains in the garden of Berkeley Square—these were two of Gertrude Jekyll's earliest recollections. The key for the garden was kept at the recently opened Gunter's and the kind man who gave the children the key also gave them the pink or white sweets. The daisy chains caused many difficulties—the loop often split down the stem too far when the pin, which was supposed to make the hole just the right size for the stalk of the next daisy to go through, slipped, causing the flower to fall out. When it was not hot enough to sit in the Berkeley Square garden, smelling the newly cut grass which had been scythed in the early morning, the children went for walks in Green Park. Here the main attraction was the dandelions—bright, sunny, golden flowers with a strange scent. And so, although a London child until she was nearly five years old, Gertrude Jekyll's first memories were country ones (Plate 3).

Her family moved from the Grafton Street house to their new home in the unspoilt country of West Surrey in 1848. It was called Bramley House, and was situated about three miles south-east of Guildford. In a description written years later she speaks of 'biggish spaces of garden and shrubbery and two ponds . . .'. In one of the ponds there was a 'sort of enchanted land. It had some great poplars growing on it, and a tangle of undergrowth. Some of this came down and dipped into the water, and here the moorhens built.'[1]

There were few restrictions and her true contact with nature and with country people began. There were, of course, still some of the refinements of a girl growing up against a solid Victorian background, but

[1] *Children and Gardens*, by Gertrude Jekyll. Country Life, new edition 1933, pp. 2–3.

there was also the freedom of the countryside. Her sister was seven years older and when her four brothers went away to school she was almost like an only child. 'There was a dear old pony Toby and the dog Crim, and we three used to wander away into the woods and heaths and along all the little lands and by-paths of our beautiful country.'[1]

Although she was alone a great deal she was not a lonely child. She had unrivalled opportunity for exploring unspoilt country, which many children today would envy, and it was an opportunity of which she made full use. Two ponds, a meadow with a deep, damp ditch, an island in one of the ponds, a quick-running stream which ran into a mill-pond after tumbling down in a cascade, little lanes and by-paths —what chances for adventure and discovery.

Some of her most exciting exploits were undertaken with the village people whom she came to love and who loved her. There was the carpenter whose shop she often visited, where she used to watch the planing of floor boards, listen to the shrill noise of the plane and sniff the intriguing smell of the sawdust. The carrier who brought their parcels from Guildford station in a dogcart and the saddler, whose workshop was full of colourful decorations for the carter to use for his horses on market day, were both friends of the small girl. There was the wharfinger who taught her to fish in the canal with a cast-net, whose lessons might prove too exciting if her enthusiasm led her to take up a perilous position on the edge of a muddy bank.

She was not only learning about the ways of the countryside, making friends with the country people, finding out about birds, getting to know where certain flowers could be found, climbing trees and collecting wasps' nests after dark; she was also learning to make herself useful. Washing day, for instance, in the middle 'fifties was something of an undertaking in the country. Water had to be drawn from the well, and using large amounts such as would be required for the weekly wash entailed a great deal of extra work. And so she and her sister would visit the cottages on washdays, going inside and helping with the babies and collecting sticks for the fires to heat the water.

About this time an intelligent governess gave her a copy of *Flowers of the Field*, by the Rev. C. A. Johns. 'For many years I had no one to advise me (I was still quite small) how to use the book, or how to get to know (though it stared me in the face) how the plants were in large related families, and I had not the sense to do it for myself, nor to learn the introductory botanical part, which would have saved much trouble afterwards; but when I brought home my flowers I would take them

[1] *Children and Gardens*, p. 2.

one by one and just turn over the pages till I came to the picture that looked something like. But in this way I got a knowledge of individuals. . . . I always think of that book as the most precious gift I ever received.'[1]

In recommending it to children she wrote: 'This is not a book of garden flowers but of wild flowers; but, if I were to try and think of the three books that throughout my life have given me most pleasure and profit, this would be one of them.'[2] She wore one copy out completely, and later on possessed two more, always keeping one close at hand for reference. (Perhaps it is worth noting that two of the most scholarly writers of contemporary literature on flowers mention this book with gratitude. Miss Alice Coats in *Flowers and their Histories* writes of 'the Rev. C. A. Johns's classic' and Mr Andrew Young records his use of it for making his first lists in *A Retrospect of Flowers*.)

Up to the age of twelve, her summer holidays were often spent on the Isle of Wight. Describing, again to children, one of these holidays and comparing it with conditions probably fifty years later, she wrote indignantly: 'How happy we are nowadays that we can be allowed the comfort of going barefoot. Do you know, when I was a child we did not even paddle when we were at the seaside; that delight had not been invented. . . . It is true we had wooden spades, and made moated castles, when the incoming tide first filled the moat and then melted the castle, but it was all done in shoes and stockings.'[3] (Plate 4).

Then came the first holiday abroad (she was twelve when the family went to Bavaria) and in letters from her father she was described as an excellent traveller and speaking so much in German that it seemed like her native tongue. She had been encouraged in languages by her governess, and her background at home was intellectual and artistic. She was greatly interested in music, drawing and painting, and in Greek art.

Her family can be traced back to the sixteenth century, but probably one of her most important ancestors was her grandfather, Joseph Jekyll (1753–1837), who was elected a Fellow of the Royal Society of Arts (Plate 1). This seems to be significant with regard to his granddaughter's interests and talents. He was also a founder of the Athenaeum Club, a politician, a barrister, and was known for his wit and other social gifts. Miss Jekyll's mother was a pupil of Mendelssohn, and musical evenings were an important part of the family life; the works of Bach were played and enjoyed by the children at a time when

---

[1] *Wood and Garden*, by Gertrude Jekyll. Longmans, 1899, p. 192.
[2] *Children and Gardens*, p. 63.   [3] Ibid., p. 89.

they were not generally known and appreciated in this country. She drew well herself and understood and encouraged her younger daughter's artistic talent. The classical tradition was not neglected and Miss Jekyll recalled later her father's large collection of Etruscan vases and life-size casts of the *Venus de Milo* and the *Venus of the Capitol*, among others.

She was engrossed by the country, by music and painting, and outside events hardly entered into her life at this time. She was now only just in her teens and the Crimean War may not have seemed very close at hand. In this mid-Victorian era girls or young ladies of English middle-class families were not encouraged to take a serious interest in such matters, apart from writing occasional letters, the usual knitting of mufflers and socks, and 'sending parcels from Fortnum and Mason's'. She would probably have heard her parents mentioning the name of Florence Nightingale, but the general lack of speedy communications would mean that news penetrated slowly into this corner of West Surrey.

Two recorded memories are of intimate details dealing with small tasks in the garden and the fields: 'There was a long lavender hedge close to some gooseberries, and as the bloom of the lavender which I was set to cut coincided with the ripening of the gooseberries, I thought very well of the association.'[1] And 'I sometimes had a day in the harvest-field. . . . Anyone who has never done a day's work in the harvest-field would scarcely believe what dirty work it is. Honest sweat and dry dust combine into a mixture not unlike mud. Haymaking is drawing-room work in comparison.'[2]

And so she grew into her teens, studying languages, haymaking, harvesting, painting and drawing, riding, learning how some of the village trades were done, enjoying music, helping the cottagers, watching the water in the ponds and stream, and noticing the things of nature all round her.

The year 1861 was an important one for Gertrude Jekyll. At seventeen she was an intelligent, cultured young woman, with a mind of her own, an interest in almost everyone and everything, and a good sense of humour. She was also dauntless in the face of opposition to anything she particularly wanted to do. She had already shown considerable cunning over the small point of not being interrupted when she was engrossed in something interesting. In the garden of Bramley House she had a hut of her own where she painted, read, studied and wrote.

[1] *Gardening Illustrated*, 27th August, 1927.
[2] *Old West Surrey*, by Gertrude Jekyll, Longmans.

Discovering that her father was allergic to the crunching noise made by treading on cinders she laid the path from the house to her hut with quantities of them. This was an insurance against interruption, at any rate to a certain extent.

She is reported, too, as coming down to breakfast on more than one occasion with a fine disregard for the conventions of dress, being without her boots. They had been thrown out of the window at the nightingales which had awakened her too early.

She now took a characteristically intrepid step for a young lady at this time—she enrolled as a student at the Kensington School of Art, where she studied for two years (Plate 5). The fact that her mother was an artist as well as a musician must have made the situation an easier one than for most daughters leaving school. It is only when one considers the ideas of the day that one feels admiration for her determination, and also delight that her family recognised her talent and encouraged it. Fashions and ideas were changing in the eighteen-sixties, but the world of painting, especially for young women, was still regarded with some suspicion. The more usual pursuits were accepted— embroidery, recitations and the reading of poetry, the pressing of wild flowers collected on nature walks, piano-playing and singing—but to study art seriously was enlightened and also unusual.

There were various conventions about using colour—if it was too bright it might almost be described as sinful. There was the case of an R.A. who would not allow his family to use chalk or paint on a Sunday and only after some difficulty with his conscience gave his permission for the use of a pencil. Then ideas changed and the use of black came in for criticism. Other restrictions referred to unmarried male students under twenty not being allowed to study the female nude, and there was the case of the modest lady at an afternoon class who 'could not conscientiously attend the school so long as the statuary stood in unabashed nakedness. . . . she sent a request to the committee that those of the male figures which were so shocking to behold should be covered, therefore to conciliate the lady student the master was requested to have the penis of each of the offending statues cut off and one of the students was set to model a leaf to cover the demolished parts —a proceeding that called forth the indignation of the male students and the remonstrances of even the lady students.'[1]

In 1853 Queen Victoria had been shown studies in the nude by Mulready and surprised everyone by wanting to buy one. She was expected to be shocked.

[1] *York School of Design*, MS. History by J. W. Knowles.

These were some of the ideas of the times and for Gertrude Jekyll there was also the problem of travel, since her home was in the depths of the country. The introduction of railways had helped, but many lines were not yet developed and speed was not always the first consideration. We find Mr Thackeray remarking gratefully that 'even a journey on the Eastern Counties must have an end at last', and of this line the story went round that a strapping youth of sixteen, detected travelling half-price, declared that he had been under twelve when the train started.

It was not the simple matter that it is today for a young woman to study art.

Now there came the next event of importance: 'When I was just grown up, though still in my late teens, I had the great advantage of going with friends to the near East—the Greek Islands, Constantinople, Smyrna, and Athens, with several weeks in Rhodes.'[1]

This was a great turning point, partly because of her destination and partly because of the friends whom she accompanied—the Charles Newtons, married at St Michael's, Chester Square, in April, 1861. He was the distinguished Orientalist and excavator of Halicarnassus, Keeper of the Greek and Roman Antiquities at the British Museum, and a friend of Gertrude's father. Mary Newton, herself an artist, was some years younger than her husband. She was the daughter of Joseph Severn, the painter, friend and companion of Keats. She had learnt drawing at home copying the engravings of Dürer and portraits by George Richmond. She studied in Paris under Ary Scheffer and on her return was commissioned to do portraits of the Royal family. She exhibited at the Royal Academy on three occasions and later illustrated her husband's lectures and books at the British Museum, making sketches for him when travelling in Greece and Asia Minor. She was closely linked with Ruskin—her brother, Arthur Severn, was his life-long friend and her husband was his contemporary at Oxford. And so Gertrude, who had been a fervent follower of Ruskin through the schoolroom, was now moving into his circle, and was becoming an intimate friend of the Charles Newtons. Every connection seemed at this time to lead towards painting. The value of her art training could now be felt, and the beginnings of Greek art learnt at home prepared her for this visit to the Greek Islands. Charles Newton had discovered the site of the Mausoleum of Halicarnassus on the coast of Asia Minor, about the time of the Crimea, and was writing a book, *Travels and Discoveries in the Levant*. He wished to visit some fresh excavations of

[1] *Gardening Illustrated*, 27th August, 1927.

Hellenic remains being made at Rhodes and to consult authorities in the Library of the Seraglio at Constantinople.

This journey with the Newtons must be recognised as a most important influence on the whole of Gertrude Jekyll's life and work. She could hardly have had as constant companions on such a visit two more valuable people. Mary Newton's painting was an interest shared with Gertrude Jekyll, which formed a close bond between them and they both took every opportunity on this journey to draw and paint and to study the line and structure of Greek architecture.

They left England on 13th October, 1863, and sailed from Trieste about a week later, having done the first stage of the journey overland. They were at Corfu on 22nd October, where they stayed at Carter's Hotel, and Miss Jekyll slept on a mattress in the sitting-room, as there was only one bedroom available when they landed. It was a young Italian girl called Nicoletta Giustiani, a housemaid at Carter's Hotel, who had given valuable help to Mr Newton on a previous visit about the Woodhouse Collection. Among the relics mentioned in Newton's notebooks were: 'small painted Greek vases, one large vase at least 2 ft high, quite plain, glazed yellow with pictures and handles . . . two bronze helmets . . . a bronze figure of a man . . . many small glass objects such as saucers or bottles, some green.'[1] Miss Jekyll records a visit to the Citadel and also to ruins five miles north of the town, where the drive passed through wild olive groves, with myrtles and quantities of cyclamens. Might she have met Edward Lear, wintering there as a refuge from bronchitis and asthma and, inspired by the magnificent large view of Corfu, straits, and Albanian hills, doing some of his best paintings?

By 26th October they were past the southernmost points of Greece and in sight of the large island of Milos. They sailed between Seriphos and Siphnos and on to Syra, and were particularly entranced by the approach to Smyrna with screes on the mountain-sides running steeply down into the sea.

After Smyrna they started out for Rhodes, the object of their journey, where they settled down for nearly three weeks. It was here that the two young women made great use of the opportunities for drawing, and Miss Jekyll mentions going down to the Amboise Gate for this purpose (Plate 7). She was obviously impressed by this gateway, the chief one leading to the headquarters of the Knights (both the Templars and the

---

[1] *Notebooks of Charles Newton* (by courtesy of the British Museum Department of Greek and Roman Antiquities).

Hospitalers built on Rhodes during their stay of two hundred years, before they were defeated by the Turks and retreated to Malta). She described the long bridge with its three arches crossing a wide dyke which had dried out—there had been no rain since March—and the narrow gateway recessed between two bastions. However, the bridge itself was found to be too narrow for drawing in comfort owing to the continual passing to and fro of loaded donkeys and so they moved on into the Street of the Knights, which gave more space and less traffic. Miss Jekyll especially admired the fine Gothic doorways of this street, but regretted the later addition of the wooden bays with small latticed windows held in position by diagonal supports. (These can be seen in the pen drawing by Mary Newton's brother, Walter Severn (Plate 8).)

It was at Rhodes that there was probably the most discomfort and even risk involved, though it is all mentioned by Miss Jekyll with calm and equanimity. The house was shaken by what she describes as a slight earthquake shock, but the shaking was of sufficient intensity for the roof to need the attention of masons a few days afterwards, as it was covered with large cracks.

Another difficulty to which Miss Jekyll only refers in passing was that of getting about the island. There were a few dusty roads close to the town and after that one had to depend on tortuous mule tracks, which were difficult to walk along as they were less than a foot wide and about the same depth. The women rode sideways on pack saddles along these tracks, which were usually on the edge of a precipice.

It was some thirteen years later that Oscar Wilde visited Greece, and his biographer describes the conditions: 'In the eighteen-seventies Greece was a hazardous country to ramble in: brigandage, kidnapping, and murder were the order of the day, and their journey on horse-back . . . was attended with peril as well as discomfort.'[1] Miss Jekyll does make casual mention of the Zebeks, brigands much dreaded by the local people in Smyrna, and of the fact that when Mary Newton wanted to draw one of them he would only sit for her if he held his sword in his mouth.

Prior to this visit Charles Newton had invited Ruskin to join him on his expedition to Corfu, and Mr Ruskin had written to his son: 'For Heaven's sake, my dearest John, never whilst I live dream of going into a vessel with steam in it.'[2] Even allowing for the Ruskins' abnormal

[1] *The Life of Oscar Wilde*, by Hesketh Pearson. Methuen, 1946.
[2] *The Order of Release*, edited by Sir William James. John Murray, 1948.

concern for their son one should, perhaps, remember that the steamboat was not, as yet, a method of transport that always inspired confidence; in fact, Miss Jekyll records that while in Rhodes they heard that the *Europa* was a total wreck on the coast of Cyprus. This was the boat they had sailed in and the shipwreck happened the day after they had landed in Rhodes. Miss Jekyll characteristically remarks on her concern for the captain on account of losing his ship, but does not mention their own escape by a few hours.

Journeys into the interior of Rhodes were undertaken for making drawings, for exploring, for studying ancient remains of buildings, and sometimes for plant-hunting. Years later Miss Jekyll wrote: 'There was not much chance of sending home plants, but from Rhodes I brought a root of an iris of which there was a quantity in the Turkish cemetery. It proved to be *I. albicans*. There was not much in flower then—it was in November—only a good sprinkling of cyclamens in the nearer wilds, and these not easy of access as there were no roads in the interior, only rather difficult mule tracks.'[1]

After Rhodes followed Gallipoli, Constantinople (she was there for her twentieth birthday), Scutari and eventually Athens. One is glad to know that their visit was not entirely scholarly and ended up with a dance in Athens just before sailing.

They finished their sea journey in a heavy storm. The captain would not venture along the usual route through the straits between Corsica and Sardinia owing to the rough seas, and instead they travelled south of Sardinia, arriving at Marseilles seven hours late. Paris was reached on Christmas Day and Gertrude Jekyll was home in Surrey at eleven o'clock on Boxing night.

Gertrude Jekyll, home from her visit to the Greek Islands, student of art in South Kensington, aged twenty in the spring of 1864—what was she going to do with her life?

Perhaps it is at this point that some word should be said about romance. So often there is something to tell that will be startling—some intimate revelations to do with a love affair or some personal weakness, such as drinking gin out of scent bottles. In this case there is nothing of either nature to record. Why did she not marry? In Mr E. M. Forster's biography of his great-aunt, *Marianne Thornton*,[2] he seems to be faced with the same problem. He describes looking through letters and documents and finding no hint or suggestion of a relationship with a man. Marianne Thornton sounds, as a young

[1] *Gardening Illustrated*, 27th August, 1927.
[2] *Marianne Thornton*, by E. M. Forster. Edward Arnold, 1956.

woman, much like Gertrude Jekyll, 'good-looking, good-natured, amusing, intelligent and practical, she enjoyed the company of men and frequented suitable society, she had some money . . .'. He ends with a comment which applies equally here: 'Still I'm puzzled and my frustration would amuse her, for she did not approve of inquisitiveness, and enjoyed thwarting it.'

That there is no evidence of Miss Jekyll's falling in love means nothing at all. She was growing up at a time when there was reticence in matters of deep feeling.

> 'I love thee to the level of everyday's
> Most quiet need, by sun and candlelight.'[1]

and

> 'Cold in the earth, and fifteen wild Decembers
> From those brown hills have melted into spring
> Faithful indeed is the spirit that remembers
> After such years . . .'[2]

Love poems were restrained, and personal experiences kept as guarded secrets. When Isabel Arundell, two or three years before the Crimea, first danced and fell in love with Richard Burton, who was to become her husband, she wrote in her diary: '. . . he waltzed with me once and spoke to me several times, and I kept my sash where he put his arm round my waist to waltz and my gloves which his hands had clasped. I never wore them again.'[3]

When Meg (in *Little Women*, published in the 'sixties) lost her glove she had no idea that Laurie's tutor was walking about with it in his breast pocket close to his heart, addressing her meanwhile as 'Miss Meg'.

Not only was Gertrude Jekyll growing up at such a time, but she was herself a sensitive person capable of deep feeling. No matter what age she had lived in she was not the kind of young woman to write or talk about matters which meant a great deal to her.

There was, for instance, the case of the German doctor on the voyage to Greece. He made every conceivable excuse to talk to her, popping up all over the place. She found him dull and boring and got rid of him kindly but firmly whenever she could, but he was persistent and after leaving the boat at one stage rejoined it later, showing obvious delight at seeing her again.

[1] *Sonnets from the Portuguese*, by E. B. Browning.
[2] *R. Alcona to J. Brenzaida (A Gondal poem)*, Emily Brontë.
[3] *The Wilder Shores of Love*, by Lesley Blanch. John Murray, 1954.

This instance is not given to try to produce evidence of a love affair. But in her teens and early twenties it is reasonable to credit her with the attractiveness of youth. Like Marianne Thornton she 'frequented suitable society'. There is mention of military and county balls at Guildford and Aldershot, and of her sister's wedding to Frederic Eden at Bramley. All through her life small incidents crop up which show her respect for marriage, her sensitivity to other people's happiness and, later on, her profound understanding of children.

Like Mr Forster about Miss Thornton—I'm puzzled.

CHAPTER II

1865–1875

Development of an art training

In a letter from Little Holland House, written on 8th January, 1865, G. F. Watts answered an enquiry from Charles Newton about the colour on some of the fragments of sculpture exhumed at Halicarnassus. It was later in this year that Mr Newton's book on the Mausoleum was published. The second volume was illustrated largely by plates taken from drawings made by Mary Newton, when on the Greek trip with Miss Jekyll, and includes one showing the figure of an Amazon wielding an axe in her uplifted right arm. Miss Jekyll refers to this drawing more than once as they had to return to the Museum in the Seraglio so that it might be worked on again. It was one of the more important pieces of the frieze and one of the best fragments of Greek work. This being the case it is likely that it is one of the sculptures to which the above enquiry referred (Plate 9).

Of Miss Jekyll's painting at this time there is an entry of some interest in Vol. IV of *R.A. Exhibitors*, 1769–1904 (H–L). '1865. CHEEKY, 64 Regt., a native of Cawnpore'. This is entered under the heading: 'Miss Jekyll, Painter. Bramley House, Guildford,' and was a portrait of her brother's Indian dog.

She was now twenty-three, with a picture hung at Burlington House to her credit. Much of her time was spent in the National Gallery making copies of paintings by Turner and Watts, and she saw a great deal of her friends, the Newtons, going with them to the Academy, museums and art exhibitions. (Owing to Sir Charles Newton's connection with the British Museum she must often have visited there and was probably one of the first patrons of the newly opened Reading Room.) They were her closest friends and must have influenced her considerably.

The Newtons were not only intellectuals and artists, knowledgeable in such matters as Greek antiquities and Roman excavations, but they

1. Miss Jekyll's grandfather, Joseph Jekyll (1753-1837), wit and politician. Pencil drawing by George Dance.

2. John Keats (1795–1821) painted by Joseph Severn, who nursed him in his last illness. Severn's daughter Mary, later the wife of Charles Newton, was Gertrude Jekyll's close friend and her companion on her visit to the Greek Islands.

3. The Green Park in the early nineteenth century. 'When we walked in the Green Park earlier in the year I was attracted by the dandelions, and wanted to bring them home to the nursery.'

4. *Scene at Sand-bath* by John Leech (1817–64). '...when I was a child we did not even paddle when we were at the seaside; that delight had not been invented. We went to bathe in a horrible bathing machine; ...it is true we had wooden spades and made moated castles ... but it was all done in shoes and stockings.'

were both endowed with a delight in life and an enjoyment of small, everyday incidents. Mary Newton could draw and understand figures from the frieze of the Mausoleum, but she could also draw incidents from her married life under the title *Caricatures of Ourselves, 1857–1866*, which shared an exhibition years later with drawings by Max Beerbohm. This was held at the Oxford Arts Club, in Broad Street, in November, 1922, and Mary Newton's work was divided into 'frames'. It was difficult to make a selection—they all sounded interesting and amusing. But here are Frames III and IV which give an indication, as well as any, of the streak of comedy in her character:

Frame III

12. M.S. makes C.T.N.'s mother feel happier.
13. B.M. Portland Vase room. M.S. draws the Calymus bronze for C.T.N.
14. C.T.N. and M.N. become so wise. He has taught her to read Greek.
15. Arthur [Severn] takes to reading poetry with M.S. He is anxious to study Shakespeare.
16. C.T.N. is cross: and won't let M.N. talk to him. He says he is tired of 'being silly'.

Frame IV (74, Gower Street.)

17. Furnishing.
18.   ”
19. M.N. can't make the balance come right.
20. The fault of being too learned.

(M.S. is before marriage—Mary Severn, and M.N. after.)

It is obvious from her reputation as an artist that the work would be of a high standard, but the captions alone show an alert and lively mind, a quick sense of comedy and an ability to appreciate the small incidents of domestic life. She was a very human person.

Charles Newton, having known Ruskin from Oxford days, went about a good deal with the Ruskins in the early days of their marriage some years before his own—and Effie often mentions his wit and brilliance in her letters from Denmark Hill. She found him an excellent companion—he was with her for the opening of the Great Exhibition in Hyde Park and was invited to share their box at Covent Garden to hear Jenny Lind. His lectures on Greek Art in the

British Institution must have been far from dry, as it is reported that 'all the pretty women in London come to hear him . . .'.[1]

Ruskin was often at the British Museum studying drawings, marbles and coins—he sometimes illustrated his Greek lectures with coins. Newton was either directing operations for his expeditions, lecturing or working on his books. 'I have seen Newton in town, who is busy giving long names to brass farthings, and putting them in the British Museum', Ruskin wrote to a friend, Edward Clayton.[2] Their travels abroad together are mentioned in Vol. II of *Praeterita*. It is not surprising that Miss Jekyll should be included in the Ruskin circle on the strength of her close friendship with the Newtons, apart from any other connection. She mentions an arrangement to 'see Mr Ruskin' on 17th November, 1865.

Unto This Last had been published about five years earlier after receiving a stormy reception in the *Cornhill Magazine* under the editorship of Mr Thackeray. It is likely that Miss Jekyll would have read these four essays in which Ruskin pleaded for state factories as well as private enterprise, more education for the young, and provision for the unemployed and the old. Her appreciation of his ideas and his writings had grown with her from the schoolroom and this meeting, the first of many others, was an event of some significance. *The Stones of Venice* and *The Seven Lamps* had been read and re-read since she was a girl. Like Charlotte Brontë, she was obviously impressed by the individuality of the author. Admission to his circle now meant that she was in the forefront of contemporary thought, which spelt emancipation indeed for a young unmarried woman in the eighteen-sixties.

It is difficult to decide which appealed to her most about him: his revolutionary writings, his worship of Turner—his sorting for catalogue of nineteen thousand Turner sketches and drawings for the National Gallery had taken him nearly two years (only one example of his devotion and fairly evident proof of his enthusiasm)—or his own work as a painter. She was apparently to be found for hours on end copying the works of Turner, so this was, in any case, a link between them.

Perhaps the greatest personal loss in her life as an artist came in the next year. Mary Newton fell ill with a severe attack of measles and died at her home in Gower Street in 1866. (This was a blow from which her father, still living in Rome, never fully recovered.) Miss Jekyll

---

[1] *The Order of Release*, Sir William James. John Murray, 1948
[2] *The Life of John Ruskin*, Vol. I, by E. T. Cook. George Allen, 1911.

had found, as a student, a dear and understanding friend in a woman some years older than herself who was already an established painter—'one of the best and kindest friends I ever had'—and one who cared for her as a person and who also felt sincerely about her work as an artist. It must have been gratifying, and some small consolation, that she was able to continue their work in Greece by illustrating the course of lectures to be given by Sir Charles Newton during the next year.

Later on, in 1866, she visited Paris with her cousin Georgina Duff Gordon, where she copied manuscripts at the Louvre and took singing lessons with Galvani. The spring of 1867 was spent in London attending Fiori's classes in Grosvenor Square and again making copies of Turner in the National Gallery. On 16th June she visited Mr Watts at Little Holland House where she copied his 'white oxen'. This was evidently the beginning of a long friendship with the Watts family, who years later came to live near her home. Early in 1868 she travelled on her first visit to Italy via the Riviera and Genoa and settled in Rome. This time she went with a fellow art student, Susan Muir Mackenzie, who was described as 'brilliant, musical and artistic'. It was in Rome that she became engrossed in the study of carving and gilding under the tuition of a local craftsman. 'An Italian who has "carver and gilder" over his shop really does carve and gild. The kindly padrone put me through a piece of work from beginning to end. First, the carving of the frame, then the successive coats of size and whitening, and the use of certain steel tools . . .'. The process ended with 'the floating on of the gold leaf'.[1]

On her return to England in April, 1868, she found herself faced with a move of the family home from Bramley to Wargrave, in Berkshire. The house, Wargrave Hill, was a property which had been left to her grandfather and now, owing to the death of a tenant who had lived there on a long lease, it had become available to her father. On 8th June the move took place, much to Miss Jekyll's distress at parting from the West Surrey countryside which she loved so well.

There may have been disadvantages in moving from Bramley, but the journey to London was no more difficult than it had been, and so her art studies could continue. There were still stimulating meetings with Ruskin and with G. F. Watts and there is a note of an appointment to see William Morris, in March, 1869. It was also in March of this year that Ruskin was lecturing on Greek mythology at University College. These lectures were the basis of *The Queen of the*

[1] *Home and Garden*, p. 113, by Gertrude Jekyll. Longmans, 1900.

Air, published later in the year, and in the Preface Ruskin especially mentions his friendship with Sir Charles Newton, who probably first fired him with interest in this subject. Thirty years had gone by since their Oxford days and Ruskin wrote of him as 'a sure and unweariedly kind guide, always near me since we were at College together'. Here was another Ruskin link for Miss Jekyll, whose own interest in Greece and Greek mythology had been so fostered and developed on the visits to Rhodes.

It was about this time that Miss Jekyll became acquainted with Monsieur and Madame Jacques Blumenthal, who were well known for their weekly musical parties. Their house, 43, Hyde Park Gate, became Miss Jekyll's home on her visits to London, and here she met people not only of musical talents, but of a wide variety of cultural interests. First, there was her host. Monsieur Blumenthal entered the Paris Conservatoire in 1846, at the age of seventeen, studying the piano under Herz. He settled in London two years later, became pianist to Queen Victoria and published piano pieces and songs of his own composition, two of the best known being *The Message* and *The Requittal*. His portrait, painted by Watts, has since been presented to the Royal College of Music. The guests included, at various times, Hercules Brabazon, the water-colour painter, the Duke of Westminster, for whom Miss Jekyll later designed textiles, H.R.H. Princess Louise, talented daughter of Queen Victoria, and Barbara Leigh Smith. There were many other well-known names among the lists of guests who came to these musical evenings in London, and there were the special few who were included in invitations to the Blumenthals' Chalet at Montreux. But these four are important for the parts they played in the career of Miss Jekyll and the influence they variously exerted on her work.

H.R.H. Princess Louise was a craftswoman and sculptress—including among her work the statue of Queen Victoria outside Kensington Palace. She was also one of the select few who made up the famous Chalet parties, travelling incognito and delighting in the informality of being with cultured people who spent the mornings sketching or practising music, and the evenings in theatricals, composing poems and limericks, or singing. This friendship with the Princess, begun among the Swiss mountains, was to bear fruit later.

Brabazon was the most important of these new friends owing to his influence as a painter. He was born in Paris in 1821, and went to Rome to study painting, contrary to the wishes of his family, when he left Trinity College, Cambridge, having graduated with honours in mathematics. His father was prepared to give him a generous allowance if he studied for the Bar, but to go to Rome to study art was a different matter and his allowance would be considerably less. However, he remained determined and after his training expected to contribute towards his living expenses by the sale of pictures. After three years the situation changed completely. By the death of his elder brother he inherited the Brabazon estates and was able to live the life of a country gentleman and to devote his time to music and painting without any financial anxiety.

He painted because he loved painting, but was always modest about his work. He played the piano well enough to give recitals, and was playing in concerts in his chambers at 5, Pall Mall, in 1871. The Blumenthals and Miss Jekyll were among his visitors at Oaklands, Sedlescombe, in Sussex. 'Eight hands on two pianos would be going for hours, the floor of the room would be littered with the scores of operas . . .'[1] This was the room later decorated by Miss Jekyll. (It has a large bay window and the archway over the top of it was painted terracotta with a design of pomegranates growing up against the wall.) It was not until he was over seventy that Brabazon's work as a water-colour painter was appreciated enough for an exhibition to be arranged. This came about through Sargent visiting his London flat and seeing some of his pictures; even then, at the last moment—'on the even of the opening, horrified at the imminence of publicity, Brabazon telegraphed from Oaklands his desire to cancel the exhibition'. Fortunately he was over-ruled and it was held.

But all this was some years ahead. The early eighteen-seventies was the time of musical evenings and long summer days at Sedlescombe or at the Chalet, where Brabby (or Brabbie), as he was known, gave instructions in painting to the privileged few. It was from him that Miss Jekyll learnt her lessons in colour. He 'carried on the tradition of Turner's later and more abstract water-colours . . .'. 'Light and colour became the essence, the reason of his pictures . . . he never painted an oil picture: never undertook a commission: never had a studio: never used an easel: he worked anywhere, abroad and in his flower garden at Oaklands.'[2] His house is now the centre of the Pestalozzi village in Sedlescombe and from his character—gentle, kind, benevolent—one may imagine that he would be pleased to feel that the rooms where there had been so many happy gatherings of his friends are the scenes of happiness for children from all over the world without homes of their own.

Miss Jekyll was fortunate in her friends. First the Newtons, who were an introduction to the Ruskin circle. Then the Blumenthals, through

[1] *Hercules Brabazon Brabazon—His Life Art and Life*, by C. Lewis Hind.   [2] Ibid.

whom she became a friend of 'Brabby' and through him again, of Barbara Leigh Smith. They were often fellow visitors to Oaklands—Barbara Leigh Smith's house near Robertsbridge was only a few miles away from Sedlescombe. Apart from being one of the founders of Girton, she was also an artist, numbering among her friends Rossetti, Corot and Daubigny, and had painted enough to make one thousand pounds from the sale of her work to give towards the foundation of this early college for women. There are in existence folios of her paintings, many of which are described as 'after Brabazon'. On a visit to Algiers she had met and married a French doctor (1857), and, as Madame Bodichon, became more closely connected with Girton. The move for better secondary education for girls and the Schools Enquiry Commission (which included Miss Buss of the North London Collegiate School for Girls and Miss Beale of Cheltenham Ladies' College) were close to her heart. She knew George Eliot intimately—there is a study of her in *Romola*—and her family background was progressive and intellectual. 'Her grandfather took an active part in Parliament in the movements for the abolition of the slave trade, and of religious disabilities; her father, Benjamin Leigh Smith, was a political follower and friend of Cobden and Bright. Her brother was the Arctic explorer.'[1] Florence Nightingale was her cousin and contemporary.

Madame Bodichon needed advice on the indoor decoration at Girton : 'With the help of her friend, Miss Gertrude Jekyll, she also chose a scheme for colouring for the work to be done throughout the whole building.'[2]

Miss Jekyll was making a name for herself in the artistic world, not only as a painter, but in many other directions. An accurate picture of her may be taken from a near neighbour at Wargrave, who shortly after 1870 became acquainted with her. This was George Leslie, R.A., a respected artist himself and from his writing evidently a person of discrimination. Miss Jekyll would be nearly thirty years old at this time: 'Through my brother-in-law', he writes, 'I became acquainted with Miss Jekyll, then living at Wargrave; a young lady of such singular and remarkable accomplishments that I cannot resist giving my readers some account of her various occupations and pursuits. Clever and witty in conversation, active and energetic in mind and body, and possessed of artistic talents of no common order, she would have at all times shone conspicuously bright amongst the other ladies. The variety of her accomplishments, however, is far more extensive; there is hardly any useful handicraft the mysteries of which she has not mastered—

[1] *The Girton Review*—Jubilee Number.
[2] *Girton College, 1869-1932*, Barbara Stephen. Cambridge University Press, 1933.

carving, modelling, housepainting, carpentry, smith's work, repoussé work, gilding, wood-inlaying, embroidery, gardening and all manner of herb and culture. . . . Her artistic taste is very great.'[1]

Such a string of accomplishments almost leaves one breathless; and there is one more which Mr Leslie mentions—the painting of inn signs: 'Miss Jekyll has painted several about the neighbourhood of Wargrave. . .'. It all sounds a little overwhelming and I think Miss Jekyll would have liked us to remember that there was a lighter side to all this accomplishment and industry, creditable though it is. The parties at 43, Hyde Park Gate were lively and entertaining and attended by a large number of interesting and talented guests. The meetings with the Newtons had been spiced with wit, the music and painting sessions at Sedlescombe often turned into good-humoured battles for supremacy on the piano stool, and the Chalet parties were almost as full of nonsense and fun as they were of serious musical study, painting or plant-collecting.

The pages of the Chalet notebooks are filled with rhymes and sketches which convey the light-hearted holiday spirit of a group of people who obviously knew each other well and enjoyed being together. Sometimes the writing is difficult to read—these rhymes were mostly jotted down roughly—and as the guests were given nicknames the meaning becomes more complicated. Miss Jekyll's name at the Chalet was Stiegel, the nearest that Monsieur Blumenthal, her host, could get to 'Jekyll'.

'There is a great decorator called Stiegel
Who boasts of her patronage regal.
In large type "To the Queen"
[Illegible line]
T'is unlicensed and strictly illegal.'

'And the champion colourist Brabby
Likes food only fit for a babby
Soft pudding and slosh
In a strawberry squash
And anything jammy and flabby.'

'There's Miss Hervey—she's proud of her e,
A favourite pupil—our three,
No relation of course
To the maker of sauce,
She'll show you her family tree.'

[1] *Our River*, by George Leslie, R.A. Bradbury Agnew, 1888.

Thursday

My dear Annie

I arrived here
on Monday – the weather
has been uncertain
but we have continued
to make some excursions.
H.R.H. seems to enjoy
herself immensely –
She enters into all our
games & surprises
with great zest –
She travels under the
name of Lady Sundridge
& has only one maid
with her – Miss Segwick

Harvey acting as
dame d'honneur –
The party consists of
Mrs. O'Connell (Mrs.
B.'s aunt), Mr. de
Wolkoff a Russian
who married her niece
Miss Jekyll – in short
Walter – a Benson
No one else has been
asked & they are no
one as H.R.H. wishes
to be quite incog –
A great deal of
sketching & music
goes on in the
morning – She daily

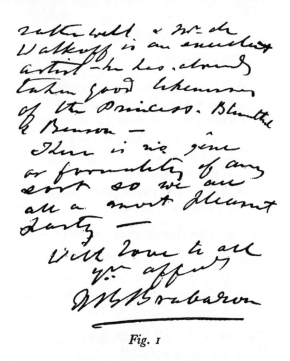

Fig. 1

The letter from Brabazon to his sister reproduced here describes one of these parties.

Miss Hervey comes in for some more attention:

'There was a little girl   [Miss Hervey]
And we'd a deal of fun
With her stockings which were very brilliant red, red, red.
Her vanity was such,
By showing them too much,
She caught a cold and had to stay in bed, bed, bed.'

'Blumenthal, Blumenthal, where have you been?
Up in my study some knowledge to glean.
Blumenthal, Blumenthal what did you there?
I tried to teach . . . a commonplace air.'

'Miss Jekyll
Went up a hill
To fetch a flower she sought there.
The price in town is half a crown
For each like root she bought there.'

H.R.H. Princess Louise was sometimes a guest, and there is an octet which is written to her suggesting that on another occasion she was staying near by as a tourist:

'[The Princess]

Will you walk into my parlour?
      Said a Fraulein neat and spry,
To some tourists from Les Avanats
      Who were just then passing by,
We will give you wine and coffee
      If you'll walk inside the door
And show you many pretty things
      You never saw before'.

Miss Jekyll's youngest brother Walter was evidently a fellow guest:

'I know a house of great delight
Perch'd upon Sonziers firclad height
Where jokes are rife from morn till night
                    The Chalet.

To great and good is also there,
To mend—and write bills of fare,
Mount hills and fetch the maidenhair,
                    The Stiegel.

Her brother follows in her train
In spite of mud, wet grass and rain.
They ask for algebra in vain,
                    of Oubit.' (W. Jekyll)

To return to Wargrave—another friend was Frederick Walker, the artist, who was delicate and died young, but whom Miss Jekyll cared for when they were both spending the winter in Algiers. The year was 1873–4, and Miss Jekyll had gone out with Madame Bodichon, who spent the winter months in Algiers with her husband, returning to her house near Robertsbridge for the summer, with him, or alone if he preferred to stay abroad. They called first at the Blumenthals' chalet on the way and arrived in Algiers in early November. Miss Jekyll was studying Arab decoration and design, for this was the period of the Arabic craze—for horses or sheiks in some cases—and she was caught up on the fringe painting pomegranates, Bougainvillaea or asphodels. Walker's health did not improve, however, and at times he felt that he might never be well enough to return again to England and remarked 'that if only he were once again in a hansom cab in London, he should be quite happy'.[1] They brought him back to England

[1] *Our River*, by George Leslie, R.A. Bradbury Agnew, 1888

with them in the spring of 1874, Miss Jekyll caring for him, looking after his luggage and bringing him home 'almost like a poor stray kitten under her arm'. Finally, at the station, as she sent him safely on his way, she said to him: 'There, Mr Walker, this is Charing Cross, and there is a hansom cab.'[1]

The spring, summer and autumn of 1874 were largely spent in London. Miss Jekyll's younger brother Herbert was working at the War Office and she took a flat for him in Morpeth Terrace, where she acted as hostess and also advised on the interior decorating. A summer engagement that must have been of special interest to her took place on 6th June, when she attended the private view of Whistler's first one-man exhibition in the Flemish Gallery, 78, Pall Mall.

The Duke of Westminster, a visitor at Morpeth Terrace and a fellow guest at the Blumenthals' parties, called her in on the furnishings at Eaton Hall after the extensive alterations carried out there in 1870. These were on a grand scale—another wing built for the family, a chapel, a clock tower nearly two hundred feet high containing twenty-eight bells and a new library, 90 ft by 30 ft, with walnut panelling. The work of craftsmen and artists from various parts of the Continent and from this country was brought together: 'The drawing room is elaborately decorated and has silk embroidered panels, designed by Miss Jekyll, and executed by the Royal School of Art Needlework at South Kensington. The chimney piece was executed in Rome in 1868. The ante-drawing room is embellished with paintings of birds, by Marks; and the ante-dining room contains portraits . . . by Gainsboro' and others; and two fine Turners of Conway and Dunstanborough Castles. The dining room has a fine old chimney piece from a palace in Genoa . . .'[2]

The work for Eaton Hall went on throughout the winter and in 1875 the Duke of Westminster was writing to ask her to undertake the responsibility for the whole of the furnishing and to give her advice generally. In January of this year she visited William Robinson at the office of his magazine *The Garden* at 37, Southampton Street, Covent Garden. The first issue had come out in November, 1871, and already the contributors included many well-known names: Canon Ellacombe, Dean Hole, Oliver Wendell Holmes, James Britten and Ruskin. (On 3rd February, 1872, an article by Ruskin was printed, entitled 'North and South', which gave the physical characteristics of countries, birds and animals.)

[1] *Our River.*

[2] *The History of the County Palatine and City of Chester*, by George Ormerod, 1882.

In June, 1875, her recent friendship with poor Frederick Walker came to an end. He died at the age of thirty-five from an acute attack of inflammation of the lungs. He must have been much loved by the fishermen round Bray, Henley and Wargrave, and seems to have won the same local popularity and affection as Stanley Spencer, about eighty years later, among the people whom he painted. 'Not an eye was dry amongst the many artistic friends who surrounded, of their own accord, his humble grave in Cookham churchyard.'[1]

Miss Jekyll's family never became completely reconciled to the move from West Surrey into Berkshire, and her own Wargrave days were probably best supported by the fact that much of her time was spent away from home.

[1] *Our River.*

CHAPTER III

1875–1890

Years of important friendships and travel—
Greater artistic ouput—Meeting with Lutyens

Soon there was to be a move once more of the family home—this time from Berkshire back to Miss Jekyll's beloved West Surrey. The move, occasioned by the death of her father in 1876, took place within a year. The family had by this time been reduced to three owing to the marriages of the elder brothers and her sister Carry, and their 'intermediate' Wargrave house was now too big for them.

The selection of Munstead Heath, near Godalming, was made for various reasons, one being that it was reasonably near to Bramley House, their old home, and another that it was accessible to London from Godalming station, through which the new line to Portsmouth had recently been constructed, giving good services.

The easy accessibility of the house itself was questionable. It is described as being built on a site of heathland and open common, overrun with bracken, frequented by gipsies and not unknown to footpads and smugglers. Mrs Jekyll's friends were concerned about the remoteness of the situation, but this was, of course, part of the attraction for the Jekylls. There were a good many practical difficulties to be dealt with in the building of a house in the 'seventies, especially one far out in the country. Water was only found at a great depth and there were no roads near the site. Stones for the building had to be brought on the backs of donkeys. Transport generally was speeding up, but travel was still a leisurely matter in country districts. Horse-drawn vehicles were the usual means of getting about, although bicycles were soon to put in their appearance and in a few years' time the early motor-cars would cover the hawthorn hedges with powdery white dust.

While building operations were going on they found a temporary home in Bramley at a convenient distance from the site. But though she was interested in the new house and delighted at the prospect of moving back into Surrey, Miss Jekyll did not miss her visits abroad at this time. A few months after her father's death she spent another holiday at the Chalet on her way out to Venice and Ravenna.

It was one September day during this visit that she met Ruskin walking across the Piazza. He was living in Venice until June of the following year in order to prepare a new edition of *The Stones of Venice*, while also studying Carpaccio, painting 'the vista of Canal to Murano' and attacking what he described as 'the assassination of St Mark's'. Structural repairs had been carried out since 1840 and Ruskin realised their necessity, but it was the style of the restoration which he attacked. A protest was organised in England by William Morris and Burne-Jones, signed by Mr Gladstone and Mr Disraeli, and it was said that the 'roaring of the British Lion had saved the lion of St Mark's'.[1] But Ruskin had appealed in a pamphlet drawn up by the Venetian, Count Zorzi, and it was felt in Venice that it was this pamphlet which halted the Italian Government in their works of restoration. As a result a committee was formed to consider the whole question and its report completely vindicated the ideas of Ruskin and the Count. The old marbles of St Mark's were safe.

But the committee on the Restoration of St Mark's was not formed immediately, and its judgment not given until March, 1880. Meanwhile Miss Jekyll had returned home after her autumn visit to Venice in 1876. During the year 1877, while the new house on Munstead Heath was being constructed, there was much moving of plants from Wargrave, visits to Madame Bodichon who had now become seriously ill, and in July she was sketching at the Slade School. Miss Jekyll's expeditions to Sedlescombe were interrupted, as Brabby had gone on the third Nile tour to continue his Algerian paintings. In the autumn fruit trees and plants were being moved to the new Munstead garden from Wargrave, and in September of the following year the house was ready and the move took place. Miss Jekyll was now nearly thirty-five, unmarried, but with many important friendships begun and many talents developed.

Although the Munstead house was new and the garden almost unmade, it was like coming home. In a letter to Mr Leslie at Wargrave she wrote later: 'It is quite true that I never cared for that part of the country, but I was quite sensible to its beauties. I admired it, but had no sympathy with it. . . . All my younger life was spent in Surrey with its great tracts of wood and heathland, beautiful wild ground and soil of

[1] 3rd Annual Meeting and Report of the Society for Protection of Ancient Buildings.

bright yellow sand and rock. The eight years I lived in Berkshire were just so long a time of what felt like exile—a perpetual homesickness and inability to be acclimatised. You see, I only hated Berkshire because it was not Surrey, and chalk because it was not sand, just as poor Walker, when he grew ill and wretched, hated Algiers because it was not Bayswater.'[1]

During the next few years Gertrude Jekyll was kept busy settling into Munstead with interests both inside and out, and continuing at the same time most of her other occupations and activities. Some of her artistic ventures up to now included a painting hung in Burlington House, illustrations for a course of British lectures on Greece, carving and gilding studied in Rome and singing in Paris, interior decorating for Girton, for Eaton Hall and houses of friends, designs for needlework of various kinds, including embroidered quilts for Frederick Leighton and Burne-Jones. Add to this her admiration for Ruskin; the meeting with William Robinson of *The Garden*, to which she became a contributor; her travels abroad where she studied languages and various skilled crafts and made collections of local materials and costume; her painting sessions at the Chalet with lessons from Brabby and the musical evenings either at Seddlescombe or with the Blumenthals, and one is presented with the picture of an emancipated, talented and extremely active woman.

But was there genius here? Commendable as all this variety of achievements was—and they were achievements, not just a light-hearted dabbling, but a real study of each subject—in which direction was it all leading? Was there one more than another which held the attention and gave promise of that 'magic in the air'[2] which is the intangible quality of work that may hope to live? Was her painting, for instance, even as good as that of her friend Madame Bodichon, who now, almost forgotten as an artist, is remembered for her connection with Girton and her work for higher standards in education? Was her embroidery exceptional or were her ideas on interior decoration particularly original? Were the musical sessions at Sedlescombe and at 43, Hyde Park Gate productive of any spark of genius?

Certainly it is early days yet. But it is the 'magic in the air' which is worth hoping for.

In September, 1879, there was the usual summer visit to the Chalet. There were more rhymes and sketches and excursions looking for plants and flowers, more musical sessions and more painting and drawing.

[1] *Our River.*
[2] Lecture to the R.I.B.A. by H. Goodhart Rendel. 13th February, 1945.

Miss Jekyll tried her hand at a skit on Brabby which she called *An Autobiography. A Fragment.* It begins: 'I was born a genius—the fact was recognised by my parents before I was a month old—they debated a long time what name they should give me . . . and thought that something classical would be appropriate . . . they decided that I should be christened Apollo!' (Then comes a page or two on his love of travel —to the warm climates of the Sahara, the glories of Venice, etc. and of his return home to the solace of music and to wield his 'giant brush'.) 'What matter if ignorant matter-of-fact people hold my pictures wrong side up or mistake my *Thames at Sunrise* for the *Battle of Marathon,* or my *Portrait of a Lady* for a black bear creeping into his hole—.

'I live in London at times—There comes a dull day—wet—cold —murky—I shudder—I seize a carpet bag—I pack in a paint box—a dozen of Chinese white—a shirt—a pocket handkerchief—a Beethoven —a Brahms[1]—a Chopin—I stump them into the bag—I rush downstairs into a Hansom—"Where to, Sir?"—"To Egypt"—He understands and drives me straight to Charing X—I have to take a ticket— Hateful contrivance!—etc.'

This was exactly what Brabby did when he found the English winter suddenly too cold and wet, and he had been known to go off in a taxi with a carpet bag and direct the driver to Egypt. There were frequent 'digs' in the Chalet notebook at the search for precious 'colour', at the worship of Turner and at the influence of Ruskin; Mr Lionel Benson was responsible for the following:

> Ride a cock horse
> To near Charing Cross [National Gallery]
> To see Brabby copying Turner, of course.
> With paint on his fingers
> And paint on his toes,
> He always makes messes wherever he goes!

At home there were many orders for silver repoussé work of all kinds and alterations to Madame Bodichon's garden at Scalands. There were also carved chimney-pieces for the Blumenthals and interior decorating designs for the houses of her neighbours.

She must have been physically strong, as well as mentally alert, to fit in so much work during these years, but some of the finer details, especially the embroidery and the painting, were proving a strain on her eyes. She was short-sighted as a girl and a drawing by Mary Newton on

---

[1] The mention of Brahms is interesting; his *1st Symphony* (the C Minor) had only been published in 1876.

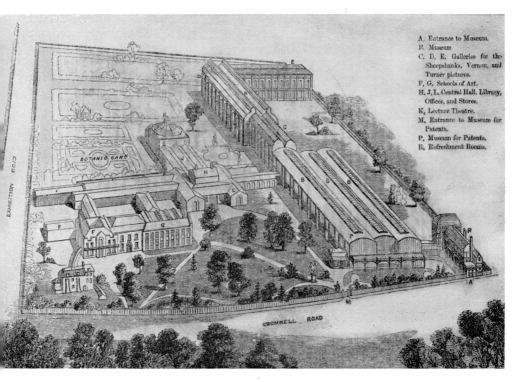

5.   View of The South Kensington Museum in *The Leisure Hour*, 1859, showing the Schools of Art (blocks F and G).

6.   The journey to the Greek Islands, leaving London 13th October, and arriving back 26th December, 1863.

7. Rhodes, the Amboise Gate. After Smyrna they started out for Rhodes . . . where they settled down for nearly three weeks . . . it was here that the two young women made great use of the opportunity for drawing, and Miss Jekyll mentions going down to the Amboise Gate for this purpose.

8. Rhodes, the Street of the Knights. . . . owing to the continued passing to and fro of loaded donkeys they moved on into the Street of Knights, which gave more space and less traffic. Miss Jekyll especially admired the fine Gothic doorways of this street, but regretted the later addition of the wooden bays with small latticed windows.

(Both these pen drawings are by Mary Newton's brother, Walter Severn.)

the Greek trip shows her wearing glasses. Otherwise she seemed to be able to enjoy all these various pursuits with an unflagging energy.

Her friendship with William Robinson was developing, perhaps on account of articles written for his journal *The Garden*. In 1879 his contributors included William Morris on 'The Art of the Future', Edward Woodall of Scarborough, the Rev. Wolley Dod and Dean Hole, later Dean of Rochester. It was the latter who had introduced Miss Jekyll to Edward Woodall some years before. They became friends and Mr Woodall stayed with her mother in the early days of the Munstead garden. He describes Miss Jekyll's interest and work in it, and pleasure in cutting out the woodland paths through the wilderness of silver birches and undergrowth. In 1880 William Robinson visited the Munstead garden, also brought by Canon Hole. Her near neighbour was now G. F. Wilson, whose property has since become well known as the Royal Horticultural Society's gardens at Wisley.

There may have been visits to Sedlescombe again in the early summer of 1880, but these are not recorded. In late August Brabazon was away himself on a short tour of northern France with Ruskin and Arthur Severn. Painting and music were the two chief occupations of these three, although one of the reasons for going was that Ruskin wanted to revisit Amiens in view of a lecture on the cathedral he was to give to Eton College. Many drawings from this expedition were shown in the Ruskin exhibition held in London in 1907 and one of them is marked as being done in the company of Brabazon. It is distinguished by its unusual impressionist character.

Arthur Severn recalled a piano session at Amiens between Brabazon and a French friend of their landlady—a charming old gentleman with some aspirations as a pianist. They played a duet, Brabazon playing faster and faster until the Frenchman 'could stand it no longer, and pushing himself away from the piano, said, "But, sir, you are a master. I am only a coal merchant. Bless me, how I sweat!" '[1]

The three men on this holiday jaunt were each of importance in Miss Jekyll's life—Severn on account of his sister Mary Newton, Ruskin because she had regarded him as a master from schoolroom days onwards, and Brabazon because of his influence on her ideas of colour, as well as his being a close friend.

In 1881 she was asked to judge at the Botanic Show—precursor of the now famous Chelsea Flower Show.

Towards the end of 1881 there came a change in her close family

[1] *The Life of John Ruskin*, Vol. 2, by E. T. Cook. George Allen, 1911.

circle when her brother Herbert, for whom she had often acted as hostess, married Agnes Graham of Glasgow. Miss Graham's father was well known in art circles, especially as a collector of Italian primitives. He was a personal friend of Rossetti, Burne-Jones and Holman Hunt and the walls of his London house were so covered with paintings that they often overflowed on to the floor. This was the kind of background that Miss Jekyll would appreciate and probably recalled for her the many happy occasions when music and painting portfolios were scattered about in the large music room at Sedlescombe, and Hercules Brabazon would suddenly rush into the garden 'to catch a sunset'.

Sir Herbert Jekyll was also a member of this circle, a friend of Brabazon and Ruskin, and there is a charming note written by him shortly after his marriage, passing on a compliment from Ruskin. Dated 28th January, 1882, it begins: 'My dear Brabazon, I met Ruskin yesterday and I cannot resist telling you what he said about you. Besides much else he said, "Brabazon is the only person since Turner at whose feet I can sit and worship and learn about colour." '[1]

About this time Mrs Jekyll, well over seventy, began to find the constant stream of visitors rather tiring. It was decided that separate establishments should be occupied by mother and daughter, to allow for greater freedom for the one and greater quiet for the other. A strip of land—about 15 acres—adjoining Munstead on the northern side was purchased, and the foundations of Miss Jekyll's own garden were laid, although the house was not built for some time.

The next two years—1883–1884 found her once more visiting friends abroad: Capri, Naples, Rome, Florence, Alassio and Genoa in Italy and a special pilgrimage to visit the cathedrals of Sens and Amiens on the way back through France. The summer of 1884 seems to have been spent at Munstead and in the autumn a holiday was taken exploring the Severn district—all the names familiar in the Kilvert diaries.

It was towards the end of this year that Miss Jekyll's married sister, who was living in Venice, moved into a garden on the Giudecca. She and her husband made out of a forsaken wilderness a notable Venetian garden. In 1885 a new string was added to Miss Jekyll's bow—the art of photography, then in its infancy. As with all her other interests this was done thoroughly, sinks and dark rooms being fitted up for experiments; and farm buildings, lanes and trees, were tried out as suitable subjects. Her enthusiasm led her to get up at 4 o'clock in the morning so that certain shots might be photographed with success. An interesting commission during this year was a bay-leaf decoration

[1] *Hercules Brabazon Brabazon.*

with the monogram LL on a silver panel from a design by Burne-Jones. It was to be a present for Alfred Lyttelton's first wife Laura. ('The Gladstones spent their summer holiday of 1883 cruising to Scotland, Norway and Copenhagen, the company on board including the enchanting Miss Laura Tennant, who was soon to marry Catherine's nephew Alfred Lyttelton.'[1])

Two of her works from this period—an iron tray with silver border and a tortoise-shell casket—were purchased by the Museum of Science and Art from an exhibition of the Victorian era held at Earls Court.

There is a letter dated 12th September, 1888, from Miss Jekyll to the Viscountess Wolseley, Hampton Lodge, Farnham, Surrey, sending 'rough sketch' plans for 'the spaces at disposal suggested'. This was Lady Wolseley, whose teenage daughter was to become the Founder of a school for lady gardeners.

Since the days of the Munstead garden there seemed to be more of a balance to her life. There were still travels abroad to study architecture, painting, craftsmanship of all kinds, and stimulating visits to the intellectual world of the Chalet. But there was also the interesting contrast of drives round the leafy Surrey lanes in her slowly moving dogcart, with time to notice the country details of the hedge and mossy bank, or to get out and photograph an exceptional tree-trunk, or the growth of a root of scotch fir. From Munstead Heath to Bramley there were high banks covered with ivy or bracken, often hazels meeting overhead, forming a canopy through which the sunlight flickered and danced. Going by the lanes to Hascombe she would find the country opening out, with tall oaks, chesnuts and hollies in the hedgerow, or willows overhanging a stream. Miss Jekyll loved these lanes and every bend and turning became familiar to her (Plate 26).

The postman drove a dogcart through the village, too. 'He blew a horn. If you needed a 1d. stamp he would sell you one and then on the way back he would blow his horn again and you ran out with your letter.' This was a description by Miss Musgrave, an old friend of Miss Jekyll's, who lived near Munstead. (Some thirty years before Anthony Trollope had fought bitter battles with his superiors in the Post Office so that the privilege of allowing letter-writers to purchase stamps in this way might be kept.)

One afternoon in 1889 one of these gentle journeys was made down the Surrey lanes. Miss Jekyll was going to have tea with her friend and neighbour, Mr Harry Mangles of Littleworth. This in itself was not unusual, for he was one of the pioneers of rhododendron growing and

---

[1] *Mrs Gladstone*, by Georgina Battiscombe. Constable, 1956.

she was living in rhododendron country, and, in any case, they were
gardening friends. But on this occasion there was another guest who
was to prove of special interest, a young man aged twenty working
near by on his first architectural commission. The young man was
Edwin Lutyens, and he describes the meeting over the teacups, 'the
silver kettle and the conversation reflecting rhododendrons'.

Miss Jekyll must have liked him instantly, as she invited him to go to
tea with her at Munstead on the following Saturday. She was reserved
and quiet when he first met her and during the course of the tea-party
did not speak to him at all. But outside, as she was leaving, 'with one
foot on the step of her pony-cart and reins in hand' the invitation was
given and accepted.

This meeting, and the friendship that followed, was to shape her
life in the crisis which was now very close. The summer months were
still taken up to a large extent with painting and working in the new
garden, and in visiting friends—Madame Bodichon, Hercules Brabazon,
the Blumenthals; the winter months with dark-room work, silver-work,
wood carving and other interests.

There was a further letter written to Lady Wolseley dated 3rd
November in reply to what must have been an order for material from
the Munstead garden. 'No raspberry canes to send, as they have been
thinned out . . .'

In December of this year there is a letter written to Brabazon
which mentions, and in a way sums up, most of her activities at the
time.

Dec. 13th/89 Munstead,
Godalming.

Dear Mr Brabazon,

We are very glad to have news of you after a rather long interval.
Thank you for the pretty extract from Mary [Howitt?]. It is just
that with our dear Madame Bodichon—an enduring joy to have
known her! It is always good news to hear of her being in any degree
well and able to enjoy anything, as she really does in spite of her
crippled state. I hope to be with her again in March and to find
her no worse again.[1]

I am very sorry that Mr Sargent is out of the way, as a Brabazon
Exhibition is a thing much to be desired, but I shall hope to hear
that Goupil 'means business'.

We are all very well; my mother, as usual, younger than
anybody. I have been doing some vigorous landscape gardening

[1] She died in 1891.

9. Fragment of the Frieze of the Mausoleum in the Museum of the Seraglio, Constantinople, drawn by Mary Newton on the Greek trip.

10. Gertrude Jekyll riding in her twenty-first year. From a sketch by J. J. Carter, 1864.

11. Charles Newton (1816-94), Keeper of Greek and Roman Antiquities, British Museum. Portrait by Henry Wyndham Phillips.
12. John Ruskin (1819–1900), chalk drawing by George Richmond (art tutor to Mary Newton).
13. William Morris (1834–96), portrait attributed to Fairfax-Murray.
14. G. F. Watts (1817–1904), a self portrait. Another of his portraits was one of M. Blumenthal.

for home and friends—doing living pictures with land and trees and flowers!

I suppose you know the Blumenthals are at Hyde Park Gate—a month earlier than usual. I hope to be with them for a few days early in January.

> yours very truly,
> Gertrude Jekyll.

To all appearances the same life was going on in much the same pattern, and there was little sign of the approaching disaster.

CHAPTER IV

1891

The Problem of Myopia

For some years Miss Jekyll's eyes had troubled her, but like many short-sighted people she probably found that it takes time to discover just how short-sighted one really is. Sometimes this is brought home by a small incident and so it may have been with Gertrude Jekyll. Work went on, but in her case it is believed that she suffered a good deal of pain as well as inconvenience which might indicate that she had an idea about what was happening but was reluctant to confirm her suspicions. Painting was her first love and any threat to her work as an artist would, one feels sure, be disregarded as long as possible.

Mr George Leslie wrote: 'Her artistic taste is very great, and if it had not been for the extreme near-sightedness of her vision, I have little doubt that painting would have predominated over all her other talents.'[1]

However, in the summer of 1891 she was prevailed upon to consult the famous eye specialist Pagenstecher of Weisbaden. The result must have seemed disastrous at the time, although in later life she acknowledged a certain debt to the myopia which at that moment crippled most of her hopes. Nearly all her work was discouraged, if not forbidden, and in particular the two subjects she loved most, embroidery and painting. The oculist professed to be able only to arrest the condition but held out no hope of a cure.

In an article written many years later she refers to the incident with these words: 'When I was young I was hoping to be a painter, but, to my lifelong regret, I was obliged to abandon all hope of this, after a certain amount of art school work, on account of extreme and always progressive myopia.'[2]

She had worn glasses for close work since she was a young woman, but they had failed to check her condition of short sight, although it is

[1] *Our River.*   [2] *Gardening Illustrated.* 27th August, 1927.

likely that the strength of the lens had been greatly increased. Certainly the use of them helped her vision—her natural sight only focussing for two inches. Whether they also reduced the strength of the muscles of her eyes, as a crutch to a limping man, one cannot say. An inscription on a tomb found in a Florentine church ran like this: 'Here lies Salvino degli Armati, Inventor of Spectacles. May God pardon him his sins.' It was not until the early years of this century that the New York oculist, Dr W. H. Bates, began to enquire into methods of treatment other than the wearing of glasses. But for Miss Jekyll, in 1891, it was a life sentence.

Perhaps, to a much lesser degree, most of us have at some stage or other been faced with a similar situation of standing at the cross-roads. We may have been temporarily so stunned by the circumstances responsible that we have not realised the importance of decisions to be made for some little time. The question of finance is one that most usually has to be considered, ways have to be thought out and the chances of making one's life as independent as possible by means of qualifications or experience at hand have to be explored. Miss Jekyll was never extravagant—there are constant references in her writing to a need for economy—but the necessity for earning her living was not vital, and a desperate need for money was not one of her anxieties. Comparable with it, however, if not more acute, was the anxiety of an artist who cannot fulfil herself.

She was nearly fifty years old. Instead of marrying and bringing up a family she had concentrated her energies chiefly on painting, and afterwards on arts of all kinds. She had never wasted an opportunity of learning, from the most humble job in building to the use of colour on a canvas. Her value of time was such that she could have filled up every moment that was given to her with the industry of her talents. 'And is it a blessing or a disadvantage to be so made that one *must* take keen interest in many matters; that, seeing something that one's hand may do, one cannot resist doing or attempting it even though time be already overcrowded . . . and sight steadily failing? Are the people happier who are content to drift comfortably down the stream of life, to take things easily, not to *want* to take pains or give themselves trouble about what is not exactly necessary? I know not which, as worldly wisdom, is the wiser.'[1]

Only, perhaps, people who are short-sighted or restricted by some disability of eyesight can have any idea what it must have meant to her. There are very few of her friends alive today who can recall this crisis

---

[1] *Home and Garden*, p. 296.

in her life and how she took it. We know from her religious belief, which shines through her writing, that she would not be defeated by it. We know, also, that though the decision of the eye-specialist was dramatic enough, she had already battled with this problem of increasing myopia for many years, and that to combat it she had trained herself to be observant and to be discriminating in what she observed.

Writing afterwards, she described how she tackled this condition: 'And I know from my own case that the will and the power to observe does not depend on the possession of keen sight. For I have sight that is both painful and inadequate; short sight of the severest kind ... and always progressive, but the little I have I try to make the most of, and often find that I have observed things that have escaped strong and long-sighted people.'[1]

Self-pity was not in her vocabulary. There were, too, certain compensations, thanks to her own talent and industry. She had this other string to her bow which did not require the very close scrutiny necessary for painting, embroidery and metalwork, and which would not be such a strain on her eyes. In spite of the intellectual circles of her social life— the Blumenthal musical evenings and the painting sessions with 'Brabby' and the discussions on the ideas of Ruskin, William Morris, and others—she had not neglected the gardening side of her life, which was now to come to her aid in a practical manner. Many women might have been dazzled by the brightness of the literary and painting *milieu* in which she moved, and conversations with George Eliot, Barbara Bodichon, Ruskin, Burne-Jones and Whistler might understandably have supplied enough for the most fertile brain to enjoy. From the social point of view her family could provide anything she might require, and were indeed inclined to regard some of her gardening contacts with suspicion. They were known in the family as 'some of Gertrude's funnies'.

But Miss Jekyll was not dazzled, nor was she a social or a gardening snob. She had always been ready and anxious to talk to anyone who was sincerely interested in their work or craft, whatever it might be, and whoever they might be. A quantity of expensive and rare plants in a garden, with long Latin names written across their labels, would not have impressed her, even though she was familiar with the names herself. Affectation in any form was outside her province, and she had no patience with it. The best illustration of this is her advice given freely and the trouble taken over a window-box for a factory boy in Rochdale.

[1] *Home and Garden*, p. 278.

56

The boy had advertised in a mechanical paper for help in planting a window-box. Miss Jekyll described the incident: 'he knew nothing— would somebody help him with advice? So advice was sent and the box prepared. If I remember rightly the size was three feet by ten inches. A little later the post brought him plants of mossy and silvery saxifrages, and a few small bulbs. Even some stones were sent, for it was to be a rock-garden, and there were to be two hills of different height with rocky tops, and a longish valley with a sunny and a shady side'[1].

Here was an example of right values and the importance of detail. Her standards of truth and reality were to save her now. Her intellectual training and her painting provided an invaluable background for her gardening ideas, but alone they would have been almost useless in this emergency. Her social and family contacts would have provided little to rely on if there had not been the hard core of her gardening interests on which to build.

It was to the circle of William Robinson and Dean Hole, Mr Harry Mangles of Littleworth and Mr G. F. Wilson of Wisley, the Rev. Wolley Dod, Canon Ellacombe and Mr Edward Woodall that she was now able to turn. She did not come among them as to a retreat, condemned by short sight to second best. She came with a background of knowledge and interest and love for this subject which had been developed alongside her other activities.

But perhaps the greatest compensation of all was to come through the young man who was now often to be seen at week-ends propping up his bicycle against her garden gate when he called for tea. Sometimes they went round the lanes in the pony-cart drawn by Bessie, discussing buildings of farms, and barns, and varieties of materials and their uses. A new partnership, beginning at a crucial moment for both, went on to last for over forty years. To Miss Jekyll, nearly fifty, at a turning point when her greatest talent and interest were denied her, the enthusiasm and youth of Ned Lutyens must have provided exactly the right counterpart. She would never have had patience with the second-rate and must have recognised in Luytens the possibilities of genius. Perhaps it was the greatest benefit that happened to either of them.

[1] *Wood and Garden*, p. 185.

CHAPTER V

1891–1898

*Years of readjustment and development of
the Jekyll–Lutyens relationship*

The next two or three years must have been a time of re-adjustment
and of getting used to a new way of life, but there was no dramatic
laying down of the paintbrush and a further letter written by Miss
Jekyll to her friend Hercules Brabazon in November, 1891, makes this
clear. It is written in the first place to congratulate him on having two
drawings included in the Winter Exhibition of the New English Art
Club, to which he had just been elected a full member.

Munstead, Godalming
Nov. 28th/91

Dear Mr Brabazon,

I rejoice to hear of any pictures of yours upon public walls,
and thank you much for a sight of the critique which I return, as
others will like to see it.

I have learnt more about colour from seeing what you have
done and hearing what you have to say about the works of others
than in any other way, and I feel the enjoyment of appreciating
delicate as well as rich colouring so keenly that I think I must be a
worthy disciple! Do you happen to have a coloured sketch of the
little Infanta Marguerite of the Louvre, in a movable form that
you could and would lend me for a few weeks. I have the photograph and want to do it in watercolour and if I had any colour
memorandum of yours think I could make a job of it.

There certainly ought to be a Brabbie Exhibition; could not you
get some other competent person to undertake the 'contrivances'?

Brabazon was now seventy and this was the first time that he had
been prevailed upon to show his work publicly. Having so recently been
elected a full member of the New English Art Club it would have been

discourteous to refuse and Miss Jekyll, a friend of many years standing, was one of the first to be informed about it. In her letter to Brabazon written two years earlier (*see* page 52), Miss Jekyll mentions the hope that 'Goupil "means business" ' in the matter of a Brabbie Exhibition. The reference in this last letter implies that the Goupil hope has faded, but it was in fact at the Goupil Gallery in December, 1892, that sixty-six Brabazon water-colours were on view to the public.

He earned high praise from the critics, and an especially interesting review from George Moore: 'The love of a long life is in those water-colours—they are all love . . . In a time of slushy David Coxes, Mr Brabazon's eyes were strangely his own. Even then he saw Nature hardly explained at all—films of colour transparent as rose-leaves, the lake's blue, and the white clouds curling above the line of hills—a sense of colour and a sense of distance, that was all, and he had the genius to remain within the limitations of his nature. And, with the persistency of true genius, Mr Brabazon painted, with a flowing brush, rose-leaf water-colours, unmindful of the long indifference of two generations, until it happened that the present generation, with its love of slight things, came upon this undiscovered genius. It has hailed him as master, and has dragged him into the popularity of a special exhibition of his work at the Goupil Galleries. . . .

'The sketch he exhibits at the New English Art Club is a singularly beautiful tint of rose, spread with delicate grace over the paper. A little less and there would be nothing; but a little beauty has always seemed to me preferable to a great deal of ugliness.'[1]

Afterwards Brabazon acknowledged his debt to his old friends: 'I shall never forget that I received my first encouragement and my first praise from you and dear Madame Bodichon', he wrote to Miss Jekyll, at the time of his success.

Miss Jekyll's mention of the Infanta sketch shows that she had no intention of an immediate reaction to the eye specialist's warning. But, fortunately, there was Ned Lutyens to provide a stimulus at this critical moment in a direction which would occupy her time and later on would demand her affection and absorption. It is to this happy relationship, coming at such an opportune moment, that we must now turn.

Edwin Lutyens was born in March, 1869, and so was twenty-six years younger than Miss Jekyll. He suffered a severe illness as a child, after which he was not allowed to go to school. Sir Osbert Sitwell has written of the benefits which may derive from a delicate childhood.

---

[1] *Modern Painting*, by George Moore. Walter Scott, 1898.

'Nor am I the only person by any means to have found a physical crisis of this kind helpful to development. For example, I once asked Sir Edwin Lutyens, who was one of thirteen children, whether any other member of his family shared his genius or had found a similar direction for their gifts. He replied, "No . . . any talent I may have was due to a long illness as a boy, which afforded me time to think, and to subsequent ill-health, because I was not allowed to play games, and so had to teach myself, for my enjoyment, to use my eyes instead of my feet. My brothers hadn't the same advantage. . . ." '[1]

This illness also meant that he saw a good deal of his mother, perhaps more than anyone else, and her influence on his character was apparent throughout his life. So little, in fact, did he see of his father and most of his other brothers and sisters that when he first met his future wife he unwittingly led her to believe 'that he was the only son of a widowed mother'.[2] This understanding between them must have prepared him for two other important relationships with older women as he grew up. One of these was Mrs Barbara Webb, who lightened the financial strain of thirteen children, which was beginning to tell on the Lutyens household, by taking a particular interest in him. She had no children of her own and as the sister of Sir Alfred Lyall, who had been on the Earl of Lytton's Viceregal staff in India, she could introduce him to diplomatic circles and help him to overcome his shyness, which may have been accentuated by badly fitting clothes handed down from elder brothers.

Then came Miss Jekyll. Lutyens was already working on his first commission when they met—having studied architecture from the age of sixteen at what is now The Royal College of Art. His client for a small country house to be built on a site at Crooksbury, near Farnham, was a friend of Mrs Webb, Mr (later Sir) Arthur Chapman. Miss Jekyll's part in the plans did not go farther on this occasion than making 'tentative suggestions for the garden at Crooksbury', but it was the beginning of their work together. Miss Jekyll's own Munstead garden was already a subject of great interest in gardening circles and, like Mrs Webb, she could help the young architect with valuable introductions.

Lutyens was indeed fortunate that he had come under the influence of two women who could give him so much assistance, both through their position and with their wisdom. Mrs Barbara Webb had provided an intellectual background for him when he most needed it, and in a few years' time, just before she died, was to introduce him to the lady

[1] *The Scarlet Tree*, by Osbert Sitwell. Macmillan.
[2] *The Life of Sir Edwin Lutyens*, by Christopher Hussey. Country Life, 1950.

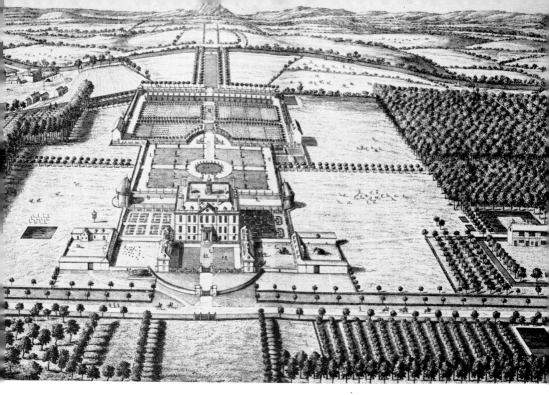

15. Eaton Hall. From an engraving in a selection of Kip's Views, looking east-
ward from the Terrace, with gardens 'above 40 acres'.

16. Coloured drawing by Batenham, engraved by D. Havell, of the south-west
view of Eaton Hall (published 1814).

17. (*Left*) Barbara Leigh Smith (1827–91), afterwards Mme Eugene Bodichon, co-founder of Girton College.

18. (*Below*) The Very Rev. Dean Hole (1819–1904), founder of the National Rose Show. 'Canon Hole, afterwards Dean of Rochester, became our friend and he brought us Mr Robinson. . . .'

19. (*Above*) William Robinson (1838–1935), author of *The English Flower Garden*. 'Mr Robinson . . . for whose good help I can never be sufficiently thankful.'

who later became his wife. Ready to fill yet another need, that of adviser in his work, to give encouragement and to train the wildness of some youthful enthusiasms, was Gertrude Jekyll. But perhaps it is only fair to emphasise that they were neither of them women who would have wasted their time on a young man in whose possibilities they had not believed.

Miss Jekyll was still living in the same house as her mother, who was now about eighty, but in 1894 beginnings were made for her permanent home. First, 'The hut' was designed and built—and of course discussed with Lutyens; this was to provide a temporary roof until the main house was ready and then to act as an extra space for a guest, storage for her pictures and an overflow for the workshop and gardening paraphernalia. 'The hut' was ready for occupation in November, 1894; she was a stage nearer to the realisation of the house Lutyens was to build, the plans for which she had been turning over in her mind for some years. She had earlier consulted Ruskin about the possibility of using English marble, and his reply had recommended 'good whitewashed walls and tapestry' as being the best coverings for 'walls of rooms in cold climates'. In July of the next year Mrs Jekyll died, after a week's illness, at the age of eighty-two. This meant a big gap in her daughter's life. Munstead House was left to Herbert Jekyll with his family of three children, and there was every reason now for the hurrying on of a permanent home for his unmarried sister, so that she might be able to enjoy her Munstead garden from the windows of her own house. Lutyens was soon to begin work, but other plans were still in hand: Crooksbury, Hoe Farm at Hascombe, stables at Little Tangley, Chinthurst Hill for Miss Guthrie and Ruckmans, Oakwood Park for Miss Lyell. (This last was an alteration to an old cottage.) Then in 1895 Miss Jekyll—now rather cosily known as 'Aunt Bumps'—introduced him to H.R.H. Princess Louise, the wife of the Marquess of Lorne (later Duke of Argyll).

Here was an introduction of prestige value. The Princess was well known in the Blumenthal circle, having been one of the selected 'few' of the Chalet guests at Montreux. She was lively, 'witty and downright in conversation' and must have enjoyed consulting an architect with such a bright intellect and quick mind. She first approached him about alterations to a house in Inveraray, but these were never done. In 1896 the Princess commissioned an additional wing to the Ferry Inn at Roseneath on the Gareloch shores. (The big house of Roseneath itself is a property of the Dukes of Argyll.) The first design was rejected, but a later one, rather on the lines of Sullingstead, had been much improved. The wing was added to what had been rather a dull building, giving an air of distinction and character.

61

This was an important year for Lutyens. His work was recognised and appreciated by royalty. He worked on the plans for Miss Jekyll's home, Munstead, and during the summer the foundations were laid and the building of the house got under way. One summer's evening, too, in 1896, he was taken by Mrs Webb to a party at 43, Hyde Park Gate, given by Miss Jekyll's friends the Blumenthals. It was a distinguished gathering, as was usual at their musical *soirées*, and looking round the crowded room he noticed 'a young lady looking cross'. Perhaps it was the beauty of her fair hair, or the delicious way that her face lit up when she laughed, but whatever it was he asked Mrs Webb to introduce him and so he met Lady Emily Lytton. 'For a time she never quite caught his name: something peculiar like "Luncheon" or "Luggage"'.[1] He fell in love with her, but his courtship was beset with the typical difficulties of a late Victorian society. Lady Emily's father had been Viceroy of India and the British Ambassador to France. Ned Lutyens had Miss Jekyll as a staunch supporter and one of Queen Victoria's daughters as his patron, but he was a young and struggling architect with no capital behind him and, as the Countess of Lytton later pointed out, was quite unknown to her.

Having met Lady Emily at various social functions throughout the summer it was to Mrs Webb that he confided his hopeless love and it was she, although already ill with the incurable disease from which she died in the next year, who invited them both to stay at Milford House. Their first evening was spent cycling over to Thursley, where Lutyens was building Warren Lodge for Mr Webb. Their second evening they visited Miss Jekyll at Munstead.

Lady Emily's account of this meeting speaks for itself: 'But we were still madder yesterday evening. In the morning Mr Lutyens took me to call on Miss Jekyll. . . . She is the most enchanting person . . . Mr Lutyens calls her Bumps, and it is a very good name. She is very fat, stumpy . . . she is simply fascinating. . . . Well, when the rain came down yesterday we suddenly thought we would go and have a surprise dinner with Bumps. We spent the afternoon buying mutton chops, eggs, sponge cake, macaroons, almonds and bulls'-eyes, and turned up about 6. Getting out of the carriage I of course dropped all the eggs and smashed them! We reeled into the house shrieking with laughter. . . . Bumps bore the shock splendidly and was delighted to see us. We set to work to cook the chops and peel the almonds and make tipsy cake, and then we sat down to the best dinner I ever ate.

'After dinner we sat in the big ingle nook and drank a variety

[1] *Life of Sir Edwin Lutyens.*

of intoxicating liquors, brewed at home by Bumps, ending up with hot tumblers of elderberry wine, the most delicious stuff you ever drank. It was altogether the most heavenly evening you can imagine'.[1]

Allowing for the fact that by now Lady Emily was as deeply in love with her companion as he with her, and that everything was seen through this rosy glow, the account still may be taken as a proof of Miss Jekyll's interest in young people, of her understanding and great sense of fun. She might otherwise, at the age of fifty-three, have resented the sudden intrusion by such a turbulent couple who wanted her to share their happiness. She not only shared in it, but she made it for them 'the most heavenly evening you can imagine'.

Eventually, after a stormy passage with moments of despair and deep depression for them both, the engagement became official. There is, I think, an incident worth mentioning which shows Miss Jekyll's complete disregard for persons or situations if her anger was really roused. Lady Emily found that overmuch of her fiancé's time was given up to interviews with the Princess Louise. He was, supposedly, working on the Roseneath additions, but there were suggestions that he was employed on various matters which were not completely necessary to this particular commision. Somehow Miss Jekyll heard of this and in a letter to Lady Emily, Lutyens described her reaction: 'Bumps rose in her thousands and gave her [the Princess] such a lecture about wasting my time.'[2]

Miss Jekyll was in the picture more than ever, and there are constant references in both their letters to what 'Bumps' thinks or says. Lady Emily wrote: 'We saw Bumps yesterday who was charming to me. I do love her.' In another letter, Ned agreed that Bumps was loveable, 'only don't let her abuse me'. All this time the building of Munstead Wood was going forward and there was probably never before or since a happier collaboration. They both had the same feeling for the use of the right materials. They both felt the importance of an honest solidity and the inclusion of regional characteristics. There was only one occasion when Miss Jekyll records that 'the fur flew' over some particular point of expense 'and I wound up my objections by saying with some warmth: "My house is to be built for me to live in and love; it is not to be built as an exposition of architectonic inutility." I am not in the habit of using long words, and as these poured forth like a rushing torrent under the pressure of fear of overdoing the cost, I learnt, from the architect's

[1] *A Blessed Girl*, by Lady Emily Lutyens. Rupert Hart-Davis, 1953.
[2] *Life of Sir Edwin Lutyens.*

crushed and somewhat frightened demeanour, that long words certainly have their use, if only as engines of war-fare.'[1]

It was an occasion like this that led Lutyens to remark that 'Bumps
rampant is an awful sight'.

There could not have been two more different people than Miss
Jekyll and Lady Emily—the two women who in various ways meant
so much in the life of Ned Lutyens. But in their feeling for his work
they were as one person. Lady Emily wrote, during their engagement:
'God bless you and help you to do great things. Don't work for money,
but only for your work itself. I shall not feel proud if you only make a
fortune, or a name before the world. I want you to be able at the end
of your life to look back upon your work and know in your mind that
all of it has been very good. Work only for the glory of your art. Be
your own judge, and satisfy your own most critical mind, and then my
wishes for you will be satisfied and my pride complete.'[2]

It was in May, 1897, that Miss Jekyll introduced Ned Lutyens to
Mr and Mrs Chance, who were already involved farther down the
lane from Munstead Wood with an architect of whose work they did
not approve. Somehow or other, by dint of re-arranging matters,
Lutyens became the architect of their house—'Orchards'.

Ned and Emily were married at Knebworth in August, 1897. The
first few days of the honeymoon were spent at Warren Lodge, which
was the house that Ned had been working on at Thursley Common
in the previous year, and which he had whisked her off to see on their
first bicycle ride together during the stay with Mrs Webb at Milford.
Afterwards came a fortnight in Holland, where they discovered that
while she loved nothing better than to sit watching the sea, he hated it.
However, a happy compromise was reached by their sitting in deck
chairs side by side holding hands, but facing in opposite directions,
hers towards the sea and his away from it.

Their knowledge of each other was still rather slight and a relationship had yet to be worked out. She was inexpert in cooking, which he
found difficult to understand, having heard from Miss Jekyll that 'good
cooking was really quite simple'. When the first meals were served on
the occasions of entertaining guests, he was surprised when a high-
sounding soup was sent in which turned out to be gravy. Her problems
were equally daunting. She had received no training in the manage-
ment of a house, she found herself shortly to become a mother, and
the house-keeping budget was not over-generous. One of the first
and most lasting friendships that the newly married couple made

[1] *Home and Garden*, p. 17.   [2] *A Blessed Girl.*

20. A Munstead group, including Barbara and Pamela Jekyll (daughters of
Herbert Jekyll), Leonard Borwick, Hercules Brabazon and Miss Muir Mackenzie.
The photograph was taken by Miss Jekyll.

21. The approach to the house through the garden—Munstead Wood. 'At the beginning of all these paths I took some pains to make the garden melt imperceptibly into the wood. . . .'

was with J. M. Barrie. Ned found a kindred spirit at once—they were both sensitive and both capable of the same kind of nonsense. It was Lady Emily who gave Barrie the idea for Phoebe in *Quality Street* by dressing up with a shawl and re-arranging her hair.

Another landmark for Lutyens in 1897 was the founding by Edward Hudson of the paper *Country Life*. The two men were almost certainly introduced by Miss Jekyll, and this meeting proved in later years to be of the greatest importance and value to the architect's career. It also resulted in a lifelong friendship.

Two more major events were still to come in this already eventful year. In October Miss Jekyll moved from 'The hut' into Munstead Wood, and the day before she received the award of the Victoria Medal of Honour from the Royal Horticultural Society. Her garden was already of some years' standing, was well known in the horticultural world and visited by gardening enthusiasts from many parts of the country. Her writings were also becoming known. She had contributed to William Robinson's magazine *The Garden* for some time. The *National Review* published a short article on house decoration, and the *Edinburgh Review* a longer one on garden craft from ancient times until the nineteenth century. She was also writing periodical notes for the *Guardian* at irregular intervals as a guide for amateurs. These notes were collected together and in April, 1898, an agreement with Messrs Longmans was reached for their publication in book form. The illustrations were to be taken from her own store of photographs.

This seems to have been Miss Jekyll's answer to the challenge from the eye specialist's verdict seven years earlier. There was a pattern to her life, after all.

CHAPTER VI

1899–1900

Munstead Wood—The house and garden—
Publication of the first two books: Wood and Garden, Home and
Garden

———

The Longmans publication came out in 1899. It was called *Wood and Garden*—'notes and thoughts, practical and critical, of a working amateur, with 71 illustrations from photographs by the author'. It ran into at least six editions in the first year and was so successful that the publishers urged her to follow it up with further notes on the garden and also on the house. These were published in 1900 under the title of *Home and Garden*.

These two books contain the essence of Miss Jekyll's writing, especially the first. She put all her heart and knowledge into it, all her experience from her travels abroad and her affection for grey-leaved plants. It is full of poetry in the writing and plain common sense in the information. It is a classic—she is at once the Wordsworth and the George Eliot of the garden.

Apart from the monthly notes of what to do in the garden, flowering times of plants and similar information there are chapters devoted to special subjects, and the book includes some of her ideas on colour about which she later wrote a complete book. There is an encouraging chapter headed 'Beginning and Learning', showing an unusual understanding of the problems of beginners, the frustrations and the disappointments, and a consoling chapter on 'Large and Small Gardens' showing her interest and affection for a well-planned small garden. 'I think that a garden should never be large enough to be tiring, that if a large space has to be dealt with, a great part had better be laid out in wood. . . . I do not envy the owners of very large gardens.'[1]

The chapter on 'The Scents of the Garden' refers especially to her

[1] *Wood and Garden*, p. 180.

66

much loved grey foliage plants. They recalled for her the travels to the Greek Islands when she must have seen clumps of acanthus by the roadside, hedges of myrtle and rosemary, oleanders growing like willows and grassy banks crowned by the tall spikes of yuccas. Mr Herbert Cowley, at one time editor of *The Garden* and *Gardening Illustrated* writes: 'It was a great pleasure and privilege to have known her and to have visited, as I frequently did, her lovely home and garden at Munstead Wood. A day never passes but what I am reminded of her, and in her books may be found the fruits of her travels. . . .' She also mentions bringing back a sweetbriar rose from Capri and the *iris unguicularis* (*stylosa*) both from Algiers and from Rhodes. (Mr Falkner, an architect friend, writes that she told him she had found it on a before-breakfast ride north of the Sahara.)

Miss Jekyll's religious belief comes into these books in her appreciation of beauty and the miracle of the seasons. 'There is always in February some one day, at least, when one smells the yet distant, but surely coming, summer. Perhaps it is a warm mossy scent . . . or it may be in some woodland opening, where the sun has coaxed out the pungent smell of the trailing ground ivy whose blue flowers will soon appear, but the day always comes and with it the glad certainty that summer is nearing, and the good things promised will never fail.'[1]

She must have been pleased to have a letter of congratulation from Brabbie, who was so much a part of her life as a young woman.

'It is indeed a joy', she writes to thank him in a letter dated 14th March, evening, 'to have a letter so full of kindly appreciation of my book. I had wondered whether it would "escape you", and though it had once or twice passed through my mind that there was something here and there that might be sympathetic to you, yet I had no idea that it deserved all the good things you say.

'Do come and see me in my new little house after your visit to the Riviera, and do let me know when you come back, in case there may then be a happy garden moment worth showing you. A pleasant young Scotch architect promises some day to bring me Mr Borwick; that might be good time to combine a Brabbie visit!' (Mr Leonard Borwick, pianist, appears in the Chalet notebook. *See* also Plate 20.)

The late Mr Harold Falkner, R.I.B.A., of Farnham, Surrey, an established architect of this time, with many of his houses illustrated in *Country Life*, was a constant visitor to Munstead from about 1900 onwards and describes his first reactions to both the garden and the house.

[1] *Wood and Garden*, p. 19.

'My introduction to Munstead Wood garden was a disappointment because (*a*) I did not then know enough about gardening to appreciate it, (*b*) I was not sufficiently an artist to understand restraint.

'In February, an early pyrus or two might be showing colour. There are trim box hedges, Horsham stone and sanded paths, the grass is still brownish-grey past the formal lily-pool and big clipped box hedges, brownish and dormant, down the nutwalk—perhaps one or two would have broken out into their catkins—the ground underneath clothed with a green fern in spring leaf and in and among these the glorious hellebores, greenish-white and cream, purple to nearly black, and brick red to pick up all the blends and colourings. How long they lasted or what hybridising had gone to their constitution I do not know, but they went on gradually becoming greener until primroses and anemones and a few pale daffodils filled their place.

'It is to be noted that G.J.'s favouring of this colour scheme was almost exactly William Morris's; purples and brick reds shading into white on a green and white patterned ground. And so round the back of the summerhouse into the spring garden and here the scheme varies from year to year, but generally begins with blueish-white arabis, scillas and muscari (heavenly blue and the darker one) to creams of double arabis, alyssum citrinum with tall tulips used as spots, but never any but white and yellow. The flaming reds were used farther on where, on favourable occasions, a setting sun shone and burned like the reds in old glass, but whether this was art or artfulness I never could quite determine.

'Once, soon after the war, the spring garden blossomed out into a fearful and wonderful scheme of purple honesty on a yellow and green background, but I am not sure that I or anyone else was supposed to notice it.

'Later on this part of the garden relapsed into dullness for the rest of the year except for paeonies.

'In the woodland a little later the dog violets would be the centre of attraction—not perhaps a big clump but making an exquisite picture. The wood had three divisions—the silver birches with one of the original large Scots firs used as a focal point towards the purple vista; the chestnuts with their appropriate undergrowth; the heath garden under the firs, and the rhododendrons separated entirely from the azaleas. Daffodils were dispersed throughout the wood, separated into their principal categories but still blended somewhat into one another.

'The Polyanthus (Munstead strain) were in the oak wood, the oak stems being bare to a considerable height, giving, at the time the primroses were at their full glory, a faint greenish light from the young oak foliage, which afterwards developed into a fairly deep shade by the time the oak had attained its complete leaf.

'The azaleas had at that time become large, well-developed bushes, all planted with extreme care as to their colour scheme and blending into one another, so that there was never an effect of excessive colour and always a most adorable smell. . . . They were grown between the chestnuts so that the dropped leaves formed a carpet when they came into flower (besides a mulch) so that the whole colour—russets of the fallen chestnut leaves, a few purple heathers, and the creams, golds, oranges, reds and back to pinks and whites—made a perfect scheme.

'The main colour scheme of the June garden was purple geranium, white oriental poppies, sages and lavenders, with a secondary scheme of lupins and irises. Lupins have been since developed by Mr George Russell, and have achieved some notoriety and brilliance, but I do not think they were ever better grown than in this border, particularly Munstead blue which was probably a species, with very large fat flowers of forget-me-not blue and medium spikes, and Munstead white, which was really a cream with white wings and thick petalled bells.'

This is an eye-witness account of some of the seasons of the year at Munstead Wood. In her first book Miss Jekyll begins with notes made in January and goes on throughout the year in calendar form, so that at any time one may turn to it to see what should be done.

Wood and Garden was followed swiftly by *Home and Garden*; both were published in uniform editions by Messrs Longmans. Crammed with photographs, most of which she had taken herself, and plans of borders and beds, the first chapter of *Home and Garden* deals with the house itself and its relation to the garden. It also has specific chapters on roses, lilies, cut flowers, rock gardens, etc. In all of these subjects she was shortly to produce specialist editions, but a précis of each of them is included in this book.

Thinking back to his first visit to the house Mr Falkner related his impressions. 'Munstead Wood had one considerable peculiarity. The entrance was through an arched opening in a wall in a stone-lined corridor, with a view of the pantry or larder on the left which generally raised in the uninitiated some doubt as to whether it was the front or the back door. Everything was always dead quiet. The bell may have made some sort of tinkle or buzz at its other end, but the result at the operating end was nil until the door opened, and one was ushered in through a stone and oak hall and corridor, with glints of bright brasswork, old oak and blue china. One found oneself in the principal living room of the house—a large, hall-like room with plenty of comfortable chairs, tables littered with books, furniture in well-polished wood and lacquer, and generally a log fire in an enormous stone-hooded ingle.

'Miss Jekyll was either in the garden or her work-room. If in her work-room she would quietly appear through the doorway on the staircase which led straight down into the sitting room. The steps of the stairs were low and broad and solid, and took up most of the west end of the room beside the fireplace (Plate 22).

'At once you would be plunged into the business of the day [he went there regularly once a month for over twenty years] usually some gardening topic, possibly adjourned from the last meeting, and then tea.

'At tea there would often be something rather unusual, crab apple or quince jelly, or some other rare conserve (and always finger bowls for sticky fingers) and sometimes even greater oddities, such as radishes grown in leaf mould. All this consideration was for the visitor, for G.J. was always on saccharined tea and one biscuit.'

Here is an introduction to the house, and one feels almost as if one had been included in the invitation to tea in this quiet, restful atmosphere of Munstead Wood. Mr Falkner mentions the staircase coming down almost behind the chimney. The stairs are low and broad and lead up to an oak gallery of which Miss Jekyll was especially proud. In *Home and Garden* she writes: 'One feels some hesitation about praising one's own possessions, but it is a part of the house that gives me so much pleasure, and it meets with so much approval from those whose knowledge and taste I most respect, that I venture to describe it in terms of admiration'. Then follows a touching tribute to Ned Lutyens and the craftsman who did the carving of the wood.

'Thanks to my good architect, who conceived the place in exactly such a form as I had desired, but could not have described, and to the fine old carpenter who worked to his drawings . . . I may say that it is a good example of how English oak should be used in an honest building, whose only pretension is to be of sound work done with the right intention, of material used according to the capability of its nature and the purpose intended, with due regard to beauty of proportion and simplicity of effect.'[1]

This last paragraph is almost the whole content of her creed in all departments of her work. She then describes the atmosphere of the house which was her permanent home until she died.

[1] *Home and Garden*, p. 9.

'And because the work has been planned and executed in this spirit, this gallery, and indeed the whole house, has that quality—the most valuable to my thinking that a house or any part of it can possess—of conducing to repose and serenity of mind. In some mysterious way it is imbued with an expression of cheerful, kindly welcome, of restfulness to mind and body, of abounding satisfaction to eye and brain.'[1]

In her description of the design and building of the house there are constant references to the goodwill of the architect, for whose ideas she obviously had much respect. According to Mr Falkner, her regard for architects enveloped all and sundry, largely because she realised that it was necessary to work to scale and to employ a T-square. It was the use of this latter instrument which inspired her esteem. 'She had a sort of respect for architects', he says, 'and over-rated them considerably as a class. Probably she took Lutyens as her standard and thought that all his colleagues would be as interesting if not as entertaining.'

Describing her work with Lutyens in a letter to Sir Herbert Baker, she says: 'He has several jobs in the neighbourhood and I have a roomy work-shop where he uses up some yards of tracing paper in connection with his work. It is very nice for me, as I have a passion (though an ignorant one) for matters concerning domestic architecture that almost equals my interest in plants and trees.'

Mr Christopher Hussey claims that the collaboration of Munstead Wood had far-reaching results not only on the work of Edwin Lutyens, but 'on the English country life ideal'. It was one of the best of their joint designs, full of their ideas in taste and material, and one of the earliest.

It seems of enough importance, therefore, to quote direct from the chapter in Miss Jekyll's book *Home and Garden* entitled 'How the house was built', pages 1-18.

'In some ways it is not exactly a new house, although no building ever before stood upon its site. But I had been thinking about it for so many years, and the main block of it and the whole sentiment of it were so familiar to my mind's eye, that when it came to be a reality I felt as if I had already been living in it a good long time. And then, from the way it is built it does not stare with newness; it is not new in any way that is disquieting to the eye; it is neither raw nor callow. On the contrary, it almost gives the impression of a comfortable maturity of something like a couple of hundred years. And yet there is nothing sham-old about it; it is not trumped-up with any specious or fashionable devices of spurious antiquity; there is no pretending to be anything that it is not—no affectation whatever.

[1] *Home and Garden*, p. 9.

'The architect has a thorough knowledge of the local ways of using the sandstone that grows in our hills, and that for many centuries has been the building material of the district, and of all the lesser incidental methods of adapting means to ends that mark the well-defined way of building of the country, so that what he builds seems to grow naturally out of the ground.

'I always think it is a pity to use in any one place the distinctive methods of another. Every part of the country has its own traditional ways, and if these have in the course of many centuries become "crystallised" into any particular form we may be sure that there is some good reason for it, and it follows that the attempt to use the ways and methods of some distant place is sure to give an impression as of something uncomfortably exotic, of geographical confusion, of the perhaps right thing in the wrong place.

'For I hold as a convincing canon in architecture that every building should look like what it is. . . .

'When it came to the actual planning of the house I was to live in—I had made one false start a year or two before—I agreed with the architect how and where the house should stand, and more or less how the rooms should lie together. . . .

'So he drew a plan, and we soon came to an understanding, first about the main block and then about the details. Every portion was carefully talked over, and I feel bound to confess that in most cases out of the few in which I put pressure on him to waive his judgment in favour of my wishes, I should have done better to have left matters alone.

'The building of the house was done in the happiest way possible, a perfect understanding existing between the architect, the builder and the proprietor. Such a concourse of salutary condition is, I fear, rare in house-building.

'How I enjoyed seeing the whole operation of the building from its very beginning . . . How well I got to know all the sounds! The chop and rush of the trowel taking up its load of mortar from the board, the dull slither as the moist mass was laid as a bed for the next brick in the course; the ringing music of the soft-tempered blade cutting a well-burnt brick. . . . The sounds of the carpenter's work are equally familiar though less musical . . . a saw being filed is no less than a torture to any tender ear. . . .

'One picks up many varied scraps of useful knowledge on a building; . . . as one example out of many one learns why bricks should be used wet. A soft-cutting brick has a dry, sandy surface; mortar laid on this scarcely takes a hold, it is inclined to fall off . . . but when a brick is wet, the moisture of the mortar at once fraternises with that of the brick, and the mortar is actually sucked into the pores.'

Inside the house there were many interesting features. The casement windows did not provide extensive views, and Lady Emily Lutyens recalls that her husband was criticised by visitors for not designing the windows to allow more. This was, of course, done on purpose, to save Miss Jekyll's eyes from the glare of too much daylight. Anyone who has trouble with their eyes knows what torture it can be to have to sit opposite a large window, or to endure the fierce dazzle from a powerful electric bulb.

She mentions particularly the gallery, which is an important feature not only of this house, but one introduced by Lutyens into other of his plans on account of its success here. It originated because Miss Jekyll stipulated against any narrow passages and Lutyens found himself faced with one at the top of the staircase. By widening this into an overhanging gallery the width was achieved, while providing a sheltered place beneath in which to sit out in the courtyard. Miss Jekyll so loved to walk through this gallery that she specially chose her bedroom to be at the farther end of it. The use of a similar gallery in later plans by Lutyens gave a character of stability, spaciousness and clear outline to his work which helped to counteract some of the fussiness for which he was sometimes criticised. Notable examples are at Deanery Garden and at Lindisfarne (Plates 23, 24 and 25).

Other wishes made by Miss Jekyll to the architect included many cupboards with glass doors useful to a 'person of accumulative proclivity', as she described herself. Also, she wanted a small house with spacious rooms—she would have 'nothing poky or screwy or ill-lighted'. And above all she wanted an atmosphere of 'quiet and kindly welcome . . . Indeed, one of the wishes I expressed to the architect was that I should like a little of the feeling of a convent, and how I know not, unless it be by virtue of solid structure and honest simplicity, he has certainly given it to me.'[1]

Here is the owner of Munstead Wood, installed at last in her own home, of her own design, with the famous garden established. As she herself described it, she had 'that most precious possession, a settled home for life'. Now that her manner of living had settled down from the shattering blow of the eye-specialist's decree, it had achieved a serenity and a pattern which reflected credit on her ability to deal with a

[1] *Home and Garden*, p. 10.

difficult situation with calm detachment and wisdom, and, above all, a sense of humour.

Posterity will remember her gardening, and acclaim it, but her character and her way of tackling what might have been an overwhelming problem without fuss, but with a practical application to work—these are also subjects to be remembered. She had been working in her garden for some years, as well as keeping up her other accomplishments, and although until her first book was published she had not given a large proportion of her time to writing, she had already made many notes and compiled a variety of articles. This all meant sheer hard work.

From the point of view of a woman, she appears to be an admirable example of how to make a life out of a disappointment, without fuss or trouble to other people. 'For', as Lord Melbourne told the Queen,[1] 'nobody should be troublesome: they should be made to realise that it is the worst thing there is.' Only women who have had to build up a life alone can quite appreciate such a situation. However occupied or intelligent or comfortably situated a person may be there are always times of loneliness and moments of despair. In a marriage, there is someone to rely on at these times. For a woman living alone it is not always easy to turn to a close relative or even a great friend—one does not wish to make an issue out of what may only seem to be a small depression. No matter how great the independence, or how well filled the life, these moments happen, and only those who have tried to make a life alone can be familiar with them.

'There are moments in life,' writes Miss Mitford, 'when without any visible or immediate cause, the spirits sink and fail as it were under the pressure of existence: moments of unaccountable depression, when one is weary of one's very thoughts, haunted by images that will not depart—friends lost, or changed, or dead; . . . fruitless regrets, powerless wishes, doubt and fear, and self-distrust and self-disapprobation.'[2]

We must all have known these moments and known the comfort from someone close at hand who can understand, though not necessarily explain. If there is a cause for depression it is easier to deal with, but 'when without any visible or immediate cause, the spirits sink', it is then that the battle is more difficult alone, and not to be a trouble to an outsider becomes of first importance.

To build up a regular life, full of interest and activity; to be able to feel for children as though one was still a child, with understanding

---

[1] *Lord M. or the later life of Lord Melbourne,* by Lord David Cecil. Constable, 1954.
[2] *Our Village,* by Miss Mitford.

and humour; not to fuss or indulge in self-pity, or be a trouble to one's family or friends; to do these things is admirable and worthy of respect. But added to all this was Miss Jekyll's battle with her failing sight. Miss Mitford's answer was to go out with two children into the fields and make a cowslip ball. Miss Jekyll's remedy was her garden and her writing, and it was through these that she achieved 'the magic in the air'.

CHAPTER VII

The Turn of the Century

Notes on gardening and gardeners, and
a summary from Miss Jekyll's writing

'. . . always forwarding her life's one object to make better gardens and gardeners, nearly blind, and always, even from the first, a little tired'. This quotation from one of Mr Falkner's letters is borne out by the Introduction written to *Home and Garden* where Miss Jekyll speaks of her 'very limited reserve of strength' and the 'real fatigue' occasioned by the work of writing the book. Mr Falkner, it will be recalled, began his visits to Munstead Wood in about 1900, the year that *Home and Garden* was published. And so, added to the difficulties imposed by acute myopia, there was also now additional tiredness and pain.

Most of Miss Jekyll's gardening was done under these circumstances, which may have been instrumental in promoting her feeling for a convent atmosphere in her house and a desire to be allowed to work quietly in her garden. Christopher Tunnard makes an interesting comparison between Miss Jekyll and Monet when he describes her as 'the most outstanding planter since the eighteenth century'. Both Monet and Miss Jekyll lived long lives over about the same period of time. 'Both had an almost primitive love of the soil, a passion for gathering from Nature the nourishment to sustain burning convictions and long-cherished beliefs. Both preferred an existence withdrawn from civilisation, surrounded by familiar, daily renewed contacts with lesser inanimate things. Both suffered from failing eyesight, and both achieved greatness through work and love of the tools and methods they employed'.[1] Mr Herbert Cowley mentions her interest in and love for her garden tools. 'Miss Jekyll was very practical', he wrote to me, 'and designed garden tools which were made up by a local blacksmith. For many years I have had in use a bittle (here—in Somerset—called

---

[1] *Gardens in the Modern Landscape*, by Christopher Tunnard. Architectural Press, 1938.

a "beetle"), a heavy wooden mallet and a garden trowel, both made to her design.'

The reference to Monet seems to me of the greatest importance. It was, after all, at an exhibition in Paris some years previously that his painting of a sunset entitled *Impressions* started off the name 'Impressionists' for the then new school of painters. Miss Jekyll was an 'Impressionist' gardener and in her own way was helping to bring about a revolution in Victorian England.

What was the development in the nineteenth century of gardening in this country? William Kent, a forerunner of the landscape-gardening school, had been 'a fine architect, a genius at interior decoration and designing furniture, state carriages, royal barges and the like—practically everything except a gardener.'[1] Capability Brown died in 1783, but the century opened with many of the big landscape gardens standing as witnesses to his creations achieved by lengths of water or wide sweeps of grass including, amongst many others, the great beauty of the 'Backs' at Cambridge. He 'cared little or nothing for flowers.' Humphry Repton wrote about the flower garden, among other things, that 'it should be an object detached and distinct from the general scenery of the place'.[2]

These three men made the English landscape garden as famous as the French formal garden and 'to them, the first great country planners, we owe much of our lovely British countryside.'[3]

There was Sir Joseph Paxton, chiefly remembered for the gardens and greenhouses at Chatsworth and the architecture of the Crystal Palace. *The Times* obituary described him as 'a man of genius' and 'the greatest gardener of his time'. But this had also been the time of J. C. Loudon (1783–1843), a man with an especial love of trees and shrubs, and one of the few great gardeners to combine the arts of landscape gardening and horticulture. J. C. Loudon and Jane Loudon produced such a comprehensive range of gardening as to be almost beyond belief. 'Loudon's outstanding work in garden design—and, with his tree-planting, his most lasting memorial—was in London's squares and gardens, so many of which were laid out during his lifetime.'[4] He was responsible for pulling down the original high walls and putting railings in their place so that the view from the Bayswater road into Kensington Gardens might be enjoyed by passing Londoners.

[1] *Pioneers in Gardening*, by Miles Hadfield. Routledge & Kegan Paul, 1955.
[2] *The Victorian Flower Garden*, by Geoffrey Taylor. Skeffington, 1952.
[3] *Pioneers in Gardening*.   [4] *The Victorian Flower Garden*.

Loudon was, however, ahead of his time and an exceptional gardener. The general feeling for gardens was mechanical, and an expensive garden, like a house, was regarded as a security symbol. Mrs Loudon died in 1858 when Gertrude Jekyll was a girl of fifteen and, as Dr Geoffrey Taylor says, 'she was, therefore, almost of an age to catch the trowel as it fell . . . from Jane Loudon's hand'. She was no doubt at that time battling with the weeds in her own small garden in the big family one at Bramley.

Now comes the second half of the nineteenth century. Gardening was passing through and emerging from the same stifled, artificial period as dress and fashion, furnishings and architecture. It was becoming recognised as a general need, not just as a form of exhibitionism for those who could afford to pay for it.

The Industrial Revolution had brought long working hours, over-crowding and small pay packets, and now a reaction was setting in. The cottage gardens had kept the flag flying, and people were beginning to realise that it was not a good thing to be separated from the soil and from living plants. There were keen individual rose-growers, there were men who gave up the warmth of their blankets on cold nights to keep the frost out of their new greenhouses, and there were pioneers coming back from Tibet and China with Wardian cases full of rare plants.

The ideas of Ruskin and William Morris were being published, eagerly read and discussed. *A Joy for Ever and its Price in the Market* contained the Ruskin lectures dealing with working conditions delivered in Manchester in 1857, and Ruskin was discussing housing with Octavia Hill in 1867. Dickens and the Baroness Burdett-Coutts were joining forces in slum clearance and detailed schemes for garden-surrounded community flats, and the Countess herself had already inaugurated her scheme of Prizes for Common Things, including an essay on rural education. She also had much to do with the preservation of fields and woodlands adjoining Hampstead Heath, affording Londoners open spaces of about five hundred acres. In 1880 she wrote to the vicar of St Pancras pleading for the preservation of the old churchyards in the City as public gardens.

This was all moving in the right direction and in the gardening world itself a new star had appeared in the 'sixties, who was destined, with Miss Jekyll, to revolutionise the formal ideas of the earlier years of this century.

William Robinson and Gertrude Jekyll both lived long lives over a similar period of time. They became acquainted, respected each other's work and ideas, and it would be difficult to over-estimate their combined influence on the history and development of English gardening.

Mr Ralph Dutton, in *The English Garden*, sums up their work together: 'But long before the close of Queen Victoria's reign better influences were at work under the leadership of William Robinson, who in the course of his long life brought about an overwhelming improvement in the standard of gardening and, as the virtual intro-ducer of the herbaceous border, may be said to have created a greater change in the English garden than any of his contemporaries. His honours are perhaps shared by Gertrude Jekyll, whose extensive knowledge and practical books have stimulated a horticultural enthusi-asm which extends to the owners of the smallest suburban back-yard.'[1] But there is no 'perhaps'.

Miss Jekyll worked for Robinson's journal, and he was a frequent visitor to her garden. One biographer goes so far as to regret that nothing more fruitful developed between them: 'Had it become more than friendship, what a race of garden giants might have sprung from their union.'[2] The suggestion that Miss Jekyll might have found in him a loving companion in marriage is an interesting one, but not easy to comment on at such a distance of time. There seems to be some doubt about what happened over his job at Ballykilcannan when he was a young man of twenty-three—though the story of his bitter quarrel with the head gardener when he ran away to Dublin, leaving the greenhouses open on a cold winter's night, is usually quoted. (The fact emerges that the fires for heating the greenhouses were either drawn out or allowed to die out, and some accounts say that the windows were opened wide. Meanwhile Robinson was on his way to Dublin on foot, where he arrived early the next morning. These greenhouses were full of tender plants, most of them raised from seeds and cuttings, representing months of loving care and attention. There is another version of this story which says that he was some miles on his way before he remembered that he had not stoked up the fires, and this seems the more probable and is certainly the kindlier story to believe.) However, he must have been truculent, to a certain degree, as many of his friends came up against his Irish temper and found it difficult to deal with. Miss Jekyll introduced him to Lutyens, and he discussed possible alterations to Gravetye, his house in Sussex. They started out on a walk which had an unsuccessful ending. 'Been for a long walk with W.R. I.

---

[1] *The English Garden*, by Ralph Dutton. Batsford, 1937.
[2] *Some Nineteenth-Century Gardeners*, by Geoffrey Taylor. Skeffington.

left him—he bores so . . . his conversation wayward and contradicts himself every two minutes'.[1]

Canon Ellacombe, friendly and cultured, wrote: 'As to Robinson, I give up trying to get his twist right—but I regret it because I think his paper does good, though I care little for it myself.'[2] He quarrelled with H. J. Elwes, traveller and gardener, with George Maw, authority on the genus crocus before Mr Bowles, and with Sir Reginald Blomfield, the architect. He kept up a persistent battle with the gentle Director of Kew, Sir Joseph Hooker, on account of Latin plant-labelling, and he angered the villagers when he bought his manor house, Gravetye, in a needless fuss over a right of way through his land for the local people. (He had, after all, acquired two hundred acres.)

It is difficult to say whether such a man would have been a suitable companion for life for Miss Jekyll; she was herself capable of anger if the need arose, but otherwise she was serene and not easily ruffled. Robinson's relationship with her was probably one of the most peaceful he ever achieved, though it may be significant that visits to her garden were frequent for the first fifteen years or so of their friendship, after which they were intermittent for a long period of time. Whether this was due to disagreement or something deeper one may only conjecture. It was partly through Mr Herbert Cowley that they came together again, and although Robinson was confined to a wheel chair, owing to paralysis of the legs, for the last twenty or so years of his life, at the age of ninety-four he travelled thirty miles by road in the month of December to be present at Miss Jekyll's funeral.

Apart from introducing the herbaceous border, his great contribution to gardening was his book, *The English Flower Garden*. This was first published in November, 1883, ran into five editions and was reprinted in 1897. Miss Jekyll was a contributor with other of her gardening friends, including James Britten, the Rev. C. Wolley Dod, the Rev. Canon Ellacombe, the Dean of Rochester and Miss Ellen Willmott.

These are some of the names which made up the gardening circle to which Miss Jekyll now belonged. Her closest companion was probably young Ned Lutyens, but these others were by degrees taking the places of the Blumenthal circle of former days. The Rev. C. Wolley Dod was a retired Eton master (Mr C. Wolley) who married Miss Dod from Edge Hall, Cheshire, and added her surname to his. The garden of this house became famous owing to the watchwords 'propagate, propagate, propagate' which were the keynotes of his gardening. There was profusion in everything. He believed that in the second year of

[1] *Life of Sir Edwin Lutyens.*   [2] *Some Nineteenth-Century Gardeners.*

MUNSTEAD WOOD

22. 'The sitting-room is low and fairly large.... The stairs come straight into the room, and with the wide, hooded, stone-built fireplace take up the greater part of its western end.'

23. 'The oak gallery to which the stairs lead is sixty feet long and ten feet wide.... Thanks to my good architect, who conceived the place in exactly such a form as I had desired, but could not have described . . . I may say that it is a good example of how English oak should be used . . . and has that quality—the most valuable to my thinking that a house or any part of it can possess—of conducing to repose and serenity of mind.'

24. Another gallery, similar to the Munstead one, at Deanery Garden, Sonning.

25. A similar gallery at Lindisfarne, Holy Island.

planting results would be better than in the first, and that in the third the plants would degenerate. And so the garden of Edge Hall, extensive in itself, was filled with plants. Miss Jekyll expressed a debt of gratitude for his friendly help, describing him as a 'scholar, botanist and a great English gentleman'. She referred to him especially, as well as to Canon Ellacombe, in the Preface to *Wood and Garden*, thanking them both for help with the nomenclature of plants.

A plan of Canon Ellacombe's garden at Bitton, Gloucestershire, is included in *The English Flower Garden* as an example of 'a quiet, peaceful garden of grass and trees and simple borders and every nook and corner has its appropriate flower, in a word, it is just such a garden as one would expect a scholar to possess who has sympathy for all that lives or breathes . . .'. Miss Jekyll mentions a visit to 'Canon Ellacombe's most interesting garden at Bitton' in *Wood and Garden* (p. 206), where she first became acquainted with *Nandina domestica*, the Chinese 'sacred' bamboo.

Canon Ellacombe was also a friend of Miss Ellen Willmott, another contributor to *The English Flower Garden*, and a close friend of Miss Jekyll. She was already, at this time, known for her work in connection with roses, apart from her large garden at Warley in Essex where she had sometimes employed as many as eighty-five gardeners. She also had a garden at Tresserve on the edge of Lake Bourget in the Rhône valley. She was beautiful, erratic, an artist—she painted roses with the touch of a Fantin-Latour—was greatly interested in music and a member of the Bach choir. Miss Jekyll generously referred to her as her friend, 'the greatest of living women gardeners'. Miss Willmott was only forty at the turn of the century—about seventeen years younger than Miss Jekyll, with many gardening years ahead of her and, probably about this time, collecting material together for her scholarly work, *The Genus Rosa*, which was published some ten years later. There is a reference to a luncheon which took place in March, 1898, when William Robinson (aged fifty-five) and Miss Willmott were fellow-guests. Their hostess was the Viscountess Wolseley and her daughter made the suggestion in her diary that they would make suitable marriage partners as they were both gardeners and both rich.

The Dean of Rochester, the Very Rev. S. Reynolds Hole, was another friend who, in fact, brought Mr Robinson to Munstead. At the turn of the century the Dean was already eighty-one, with most of his life's work behind him. Like Miss Willmott, he will be remembered in connection with roses, and, like her, he grew quantities of roses himself and wrote about them. In *A Book About Roses*, which went into at least ten editions, he enumerates and describes hundreds of roses, most of which he knew well himself, and many of which he had grown in his own gardens, first near Newark and then at Rochester.

Of all these roses, he mentions especially the Gloire de Dijon as being the one best as a climber and the one he could least manage without. He writes of one growing on the chancel wall of his church which often had two hundred flowers on it at once. He is best known, perhaps, as the founder of the Rose Show, and the beginnings of this enterprise he describes in his book. Roses were his speciality, but he was also a keen sportsman and a lively member of the Garrick Club where evenings were spent in discussions with Dickens, Thackeray and John Leech. The latter became a close friend, and was best man at his wedding. Two of his gardening friends were William Robinson and Shirley Hibberd.[1]

There were still others of the circle—G. F. Wilson,[2] who was planting his garden at Wisley when Miss Jekyll was at Munstead and who allowed her to do 'actual spade work with him'. She recalled especially a hedge of *Rosa rugosa* in full fruit, and a plantation of *Primula denticulata*. And there was Mr Edward Woodall, introduced by the Dean of Rochester, who remembered the early days of the Munstead garden, and who was to co-operate with Miss Jekyll in some of her later written work, producing a chapter for one of her books. Mrs Theresa Earle was a visitor to Munstead, and comments in one of her books on Miss Jekyll's garden notes for the *Guardian*: 'I trust that before long these articles will be republished in book form, for every word in them deserves attention and consideration.'[3] Two other visitors in the year 1900 were Mr E. T. Cook and Mr Edward Hudson. The former persuaded her to take on the joint editorship of *The Garden*, which she did for the years 1900–1. Mr Hudson, editor of *Country Life*, was already a good friend to Ned Lutyens. A constant and very welcome visitor towards the end of her life, and much younger than most of these mentioned, Herbert Cowley was editor of *The Garden* from 1915–21, and editor of *Gardening Illustrated* from 1923–6. He is also a well-known plant collector, going on expeditions to the Dolomites, the Pyrenees, Majorca and Spain.

Another friend who first made his appearance at Munstead about 1900 has already been mentioned and quoted—Mr Harold Falkner. He worked, among other projects, for the Society for the Protection of Ancient Buildings. He was apprenticed in the office of Sir Reginald

[1] Author of *Rustic Adornments for Houses of Taste*, 1856.
[2] *Wood and Garden*, p. 184.
[3] *Pot-Pourri from a Surrey Garden*, by Mrs C. W. Earle. Smith, Elder, 1899.

Blomfield, author of *The Formal Garden*, and so was trained from his early days in the ideas of the formal garden. These ideas were in complete opposition to the naturalistic gardening of William Robinson and also, of course, to Miss Jekyll. But when Mr Falkner went round the garden of Munstead Wood he was completely won over. He says that 'it was partly formal, partly controlled wild'. He also recalled Miss Jekyll's attitude to this battle between the formal and the informal garden designers. 'She used to relate with great glee the fact that Robinson designed himself a garden all squares, and Reggy a garden on a cliff with not a straight line in it.' (Robinson's garden at Gravetye had a paved garden close to the house, so that he could easily reach his favourite plants.)

Just before the turn of the century—in 1899—Lutyens had added another wing to Crooksbury, and completed Deanery Garden for Edward Hudson. Of the latter Christopher Hussey wrote: 'Deanery Garden, at once formal and irregular, virtually settled that controversy of which Sir Reginald Blomfield and William Robinson were the protagonists, between formal and naturalistic garden design. Miss Jekyll's naturalistic planting wedded Lutyen's geometry in a balanced union of both principles.'[1] Mr Falkner contended that Miss Jekyll's own garden was 'partly formal'. He went further and said: 'In her first books she seemed to harp on naturalism in gardens in direct opposition (to Sir Reginald Blomfield's *The Formal Garden*), but gradually she and E.L. came to our way of thinking and from the second addition of Crooksbury on to Great Maytham had become *Formal* in garden and classic in houses.'

Perhaps she had become slightly more formal, but that is as much as one can allow. Perhaps Mr Falkner had become slightly less formal.

This is the picture, then, at the turn of the century. Miss Jekyll, writing in the *Edinburgh Review*, July, 1896, says: 'Within the last few years . . . another war of controversy has raged between the exponents of formal and the free styles of gardening, and again it is to be regretted that it has taken a somewhat bitter and almost personal tone. . . . Both are right and both are wrong. The formal army are architects to a man; they are undoubtedly right in upholding the simple dignity and sweetness and quiet beauty of the old formal garden but . . . they ignore the immense resources that are the precious possession of modern gardeners, and therefore offer no sort of encouragement to their utilisation. . . . We cannot now, with all this treasure at our feet, neglect it and refuse it the gratefully appreciative use it deserves. We cannot go back a century

[1] *Life of Sir Edwin Lutyens.*

or two and stop short at the art of the formal gardener any more than we can go back to the speech of our forefathers, beautiful though it was. There is change and growth in all wholesome art, and gardening at its best is a fine art. For ever true is what Bacon says: "Men come to build stately sooner than to garden finely, as if gardening were the greater perfection."

'To borrow illustrations from other arts, the champions of the formal garden only would stop short at the music of Bach, which represented the widest scope and highest development of the art in his day. But since then instruments have grown in kind and compass, and the range of possibilities in orchestral combination has widely increased . . . the pictorial art of Botticelli is everything that the architects claim for the formal garden; it is full of sweetness and beauty, full of limitations, frankly artificial, frankly artistic. But paintings could not remain within the bounds that fenced the art of Botticelli, and a century later we have the work of the great Venetians, and again, in rather less than another hundred years, that of Velasquez and Rembrandt. So near to nature does Velasquez come that Ruskin says of his portraiture, "He flings the man himself upon the canvas." '[1] Mention of Ruskin reminds one that his life, spent in retirement near Coniston for the last eleven years, was coming to an end. After only three days' illness with influenza, on 20th January, 1900, he died peacefully. For Miss Jekyll, that day must have brought back memories of youthful enthusiasms, and especially her life-long worship of Turner.

With the death of Queen Victoria in 1901 there came the end of an era and the beginning of an era. 'But when Victoria died . . . country roads and lanes were still country roads and lanes, with all their sleepy charm come down from countless centuries, which the invading bicyclist could enjoy without destroying.'[2] For this was the heyday of the bicycle. It was a means of escape—as for W. H. Hudson from the London streets towards the Sussex Downs, or a means of getting about a large city—as for Tolstoy cycling about in Moscow (on a British machine made in Coventry), or as a means of getting about in the country lanes—as in the case of Edwin Lutyens, who first visited Miss Jekyll on a bicycle, as also did Mr Falkner. Many of Lutyens' first expeditions with Lady Emily Lytton were made by bicycle, and many of his first plans for houses were tucked under his arm as he pedalled on his way to Munstead for criticism or approval.

When Lutyens and Miss Jekyll were driving together through these

[1] 'The Idea of a Garden', by Gertrude Jekyll. *Edinburgh Review*, July, 1896.
[2] *English Social History*, by G. M. Trevelyan, p. 575 1944.

26. '...it was on gentle drives in the sleepy charm of these winding Surrey lanes that certain foundations were laid of an English way of life.'

27. (*Below*) Drawing by Lutyens of Miss Jekyll, *c.* 1896.

28. (*Right*) Drawing of Lutyens by Phipps, *c.* 1906.

MUNSTEAD WOOD GARDEN

29. (*Left*) Bunch primroses. 'The primrose garden is in a place by itself—a clearing half shaded by oak, chestnut and hazel.'

30. (*Right*) Guelder rose over the garden door (showing cottage style influence). 'The old guelder rose is beautiful anywhere, but I think it is best of all on the cold side of a wall.'

31. The Spring Garden. 'My spring garden lies at the end and back of a high wall. . . .'

West Surrey lanes, drawn by Bessie, they might notice the slant of a roof, the colour of some tile-hung cottage walls, the angle of a chimney, the planting inside a cottage garden or primroses on a mossy bank. For it was on gentle drives in the 'sleepy charm' of these winding lanes that the foundations were laid of an English way of life.

CHAPTER VIII

1900–1905

Publication of Roses for English Gardens, Lilies for English Gardens, Old West Surrey—*Garden designs for Lutyens' houses— Visitors to Munstead garden*

These were years of large literary output—almost a book a year—and of successful collaboration with Lutyens. Most of the publication now was by Country Life, and one of Lutyens' important commissions during this time was that of the new Country Life offices in Tavistock Street, Covent Garden—his first London building.

First—Miss Jekyll's books. In 1901 *Lilies for English Gardens* made its appearance with the sub-title 'A Guide for Amateurs'. It was the result of a series of queries sent out to thirty known lily growers by the editors of *The Garden*. At the time, Miss Jekyll was co-editor with E. T. Cook. In the Preface she remarks that many less-known lilies have been omitted. 'They concern the botanist, whose business it is to know and to classify everything; they scarcely concern the gardener whose interest it is to know what lilies will best grace his garden.'

There are notes on 'deep or shallow planting', on 'lilies as pot plants' and a list giving suitability of different lilies for growing in different parts of England, depending on the soil conditions. To the unbotanical mind there also appears to be a great deal of material and information about lilies which seems to be highly technical. But it is presented in such a way as to be irresistible and, no matter how little knowledge one has, it is exciting to read. A photograph showing a border of *lilium Candidum* growing at the foot of a long vine-covered pergola shading an extensive length of pathway is one of the illustrations in this book, and is taken from her sister's garden on the Giudecca. In her book Miss Jekyll devotes a chapter to the *lilium Candidum*. 'A plant so lovely it should be tried in every garden'—but remarks on its capricious characteristics and the fact that some flourish in hot sun, while others prefer a shady situation, or some like a rich soil while others prefer limestone. Of the Venice border it is said: 'They require replanting with change of place every half-dozen years, and in fresh soil grow so grandly that we have often heads of fifteen, sixteen, and even twenty flowers on a single stem, of sometimes 5½ feet high.'[1]

Then came *Wall and Water Gardens*, also published in 1901. This is one of the most attractive of all her books, being written from the point of view that—as she explains to children—'nothing is so delightful as playing with water'. A great deal of her philosophy is in this book, and there is poetry in the writing of it, too. Under the chapter heading 'When to let well alone' she describes a certain wild forest pool. 'Here is a glimpse of quiet natural beauty; pure nature untouched. Being in itself beautiful, and speaking direct to our minds of the poetry of the wood-land, it would be an ill deed to mar its perfection by any meddlesome gardening. The most one could do in such a place, where deer may come down to drink and the dragonfly flashes in the broken midsummer light, would be to plant in the upper ground some native wild flower that would be in harmony with the place but that may happen to be absent, such as wood sorrel or wood anemone.'[2] (Plate 37.)

There is the beauty of restraint in her treatment of this pond, just as there is beauty in the words she uses to describe it. She resists all temptation to make any proposals involving rare or exotic water plants. The suggestion of wood sorrel or wood anemone would be in tune with the woodland scene. One can imagine dreadful things which might be done by someone with eager, but inartistic ideas to a simple pool set among wild flowers, grasses, ferns and trees.

This book also has chapters on rock gardens, alpine gardens and heath gardens, with plans and lists of plants and shrubs suitable for use in these situations.

Roses for English Gardens was published in 1902 by Country Life. The book was written in conjunction with Mr Edward Mawley[3], and divided into two parts, one part written by each author. Miss Jekyll's contribution, rather more than half the book, is entitled 'Old and new roses and their beautiful use in gardens'. Mr Mawley deals with the more practical side of 'pruning, planting and propagating'.

There are now, and were even at that time, books about roses which deal with the methods of growing and cultivation, but it seems fairly safe to say that this was the first one to approach the subject from the

---

[1] *A Garden in Venice*, by F. Eden. Country Life, 1903.
[2] *Wall and Water Gardens*, p. 65.
[3] One of the founders of the National Rose Society.

point of view of 'how they may be most beautifully used'. Miss Jekyll mentions this in her Preface, once again emphasising that it is hoped that they will be particularly attractive to the amateur. She acknowledges one chapter especially written for her part of the book by her old friend Mr Edward Woodall on Riviera garden roses. To justify its presence in a book with the title *Roses for English Gardens*, the chapter is entitled 'Roses in English Gardens on the Riviera'. That it should be considered useful in this particular book provides an interesting comment on the times. Mr Woodall had himself been connected with the public gardens of Scarborough for many years, and these he enriched 'very considerably by gifts of rare and new specimens of plant life'. So writes Mr J. Clark, who took up the post of Parks Superintendent in Scarborough in 1922. Mr Woodall's health was not good, and he spent the winter months in his house near Nice, which had a fine garden. And so it was from his personal experience of Riviera gardening conditions that he wrote this chapter.

There are many illustrations in the book, more of them actually showing the ways of training and growing roses than close-ups of a special rose. Roses are photographed climbing over a balcony, growing up into trees, among cypresses, as garlands along a wire framework, hanging over a wall, twining their way up brick pillars, clothing dead apple trees, making an ordinary square or rounded arch, decorating a verandah, covering the wall of a house, scrambling over a low bank, trained through willows and climbing up through the lower bare branches of an old catalpa.

It is impossible to turn the pages of photographs without immediately wanting to order another rose for the garden, or to try out one of the ideas with a climber already installed.

It is unnecessary to add, perhaps, that the only illustration of a formal rose bed, where the roses are jammed together in a bed cut into the grass, bears the very gentle criticism, 'A kind of rose garden that may be much improved upon'.

The next literary venture was something of a rather different character. Away, this time, from roses, lilies, Munstead Wood, rock gardens and water gardens, and back to the memories of her childhood—the book is called *Old West Surrey*, published in 1904 by Longmans. This was enlarged and re-published in 1925 by Batsford under the title of *Old English Household Life*.

The knowledge that Gertrude Jekyll had acquired from going in and out of cottages and cottage gardens, from driving down the lanes in her pony cart, and from her familiarity with the cottagers themselves, was quite prodigious. She knew about their customs and their means of living, and a great deal of her knowledge is autobiographical. 'I can remember when corn was commonly threshed with the flail', she writes, and she describes, too, the hard labour of harvesting. On the making of cider, she writes: 'Cider is still made with the old wooden press. The apples are first crushed by a roller in the cider-mill. . . . The heaps of apples, mostly of the poorest orchard produce, do not look at all inviting. Many are muddy and bruised, but in they go, mud and all; and when a mug of the freshly pressed juice is offered, and is accepted with some internal hesitation, whose outward expression is repressed for civility's sake, one is pleasantly surprised to find what a delicious drink tasting clean and pure and refreshing, is this newly drawn juice of quite second- and third-rate apples.'[1] (The creator of Peter Rabbit, Squirrel Nutkin, Hunca Munca, and other friends of the countryside, who began to make their appearance in book form at about the same time that Miss Jekyll's gardening books were being published, recalls a similar experience. Introduced into the mysteries of a perry mill near Stroud, 'she was shocked to see snails being shovelled into the press with the pears.'[2])

Miss Jekyll describes the forerunner of the play-pen: 'When the baby had grown beyond the crawling stage, it was exercised and encouraged to find its feet, and at the same time kept safe from the fire in the baby-runner. The upright rod fitted into a hole in the floor, and at the top into a beam or one of the thick beam-like oak joists that carried the bedroom floor. The child was put into the wooden ring, and the rack was arranged to suit its height. The child could then move about in as much of a circle as the position of the contrivance would allow.'

Writing of horse-brasses: 'Those of a raised crescent shape are of an extremely ancient design; the lower one on the right, with three crescents joined, I think I remember to be identical with an Assyrian horse-ornament.'[3] The wealth of knowledge collected together on her travels abroad or in her art training permeated throughout her work and ideas.

There are two particularly interesting notes on the first matches and the early use of pottery respectively. On pottery: 'At first sight it is a matter of wonder that so much earthenware from the north and middle of England should have been in common use in early days in the southern counties; but it should be remembered that before the

---

[1] *Old West Surrey*, or *Old English Household Life*, p. 152.
[2] *The Tales of Beatrix Potter*, by Margaret Lane. F. Warne.
[3] *Old West Surrey*, or *Old English Household Life*, p. 169.

time of railways there was a cheap though slow means of communication by canal barges.' The mention of the first matches is made by someone Miss Jekyll knew, who recalled their arrival in this country: '"The first lucifer matches I ever seen", said one of my old neighbours, "was in the year 1839. They came from Southampton and were called Congreves, and were sold by the gross. I think they were made in France." '

These are only a few excerpts from a store of others of equal interest, and it is clear from Miss Jekyll's writing that she is an authority on all kinds of paving (ripple-marked stone, and iron-stone pitching); wells; bacon-lofts; gates; kitchen fire-places; clocks, granaries; dairies; draw-plaiting; samplers; patchwork; candlesticks; thatching; inn signs; churchyards and tombstones, and the speech, manners and customs of the village people. There is also an excellent chapter on smuggling and another on the history of Godalming.

All these references are to the first of the two books—*Old West Surrey*, though much of the same material is now to be found in *Old English Household Life*.

It is not difficult to understand why she should be so much in sympathy with the young architect, Edwin Lutyens. Most of her early training had prepared her for a wide field of interest, and her active and receptive mind welcomed other channels to explore. It was not only as a kindness to Lutyens that she put by a large workshop for him to use when working near by, or on their joint enterprises. Munstead Wood with its conventional atmosphere became for many years his second home, where she enjoyed seeing him 'use up yards of tracing paper'.

By now Lutyens was a name in the architectural world. The addition to Crooksbury for the Chapmans (1899), Orchards, near Godalming for Lady Chance (1898–9), Deanery Garden, Sonning, for E. H. Hudson (1899), Little Thakeham, Sussex (1902), Marsh Court, Stockbridge, Hampshire (1901)—all these were enlarging his reputation, and the basis and foundation of it all was the house built for Miss Jekyll at Munstead (1897).

The photographs of Crooksbury had been in *Country Life*, and his work on the old bridges over the Thames at Sonning in 1902 was described by the editor in the same journal as coming 'from the hand of Mr E. L. Lutyens, whose work, by its structural excellence in all materials, especially in brick and timber and by its good sense and good taste, has won lasting reputation in every department of country architecture'. *Country Life* offices were going up in 1905; then came

Folly Farm, Sulhampstead, Berkshire, and the triumph of Hestercombe in Somerset. Mr Hussey makes a comment of particular interest, referring to these beautiful terraced gardens near Taunton. 'The Hestercombe gardens represent the peak of the collaboration with Miss Jekyll, and his first application of her genius to classical garden design on a grand scale'.[1] There were iris canals, rose pergolas, an orangery, an immense parterre with massed herbaceous planting, and grass walks with paved edges, all designed to make the best of a wonderful situation overlooking Taunton Dene.

It is interesting to notice here the size and grandeur of Hestercombe gardens and to compare them with those of Eaton Hall or Girton (Plates 15 and 16). Thirty years earlier she had been called in on the interior furnishings of Eaton (1870), but there was no question then of asking her advice or help on the gardens. There is, after all, no doubt of the size and extent of the Eaton Hall estate. 'The gardens and pleasure grounds are formed on the before mentioned gentle slope to the river Dee: they are laid out in a very tasteful manner, and contain a choice collection of exotics and rare fruits of every description.'[2] It is obvious, therefore, that advice would be needed. Mr Ormerod wrote: 'The gardens have been greatly improved . . . and the extensive conservatories, with nearly six miles of hot-water pipes.' Madame Bodichon had asked her advice in *interior* decoration for Girton. It is a reflection on the change in Miss Jekyll's life and proof of her now professional approach to gardening.

She was asked for advice from all over the country and from abroad. Sir Herbert Baker was writing from Cape Town for advice on Cecil Rhodes's garden at Groote Schuur. 'Rhodes liked to deal in masses, as was his way, and did not understand that, as Bacon prescribes, a garden should be smaller in scale and more intimate in design near the house but enlarge in mass and wilder growth as it recedes and mingles with the natural landscape . . . Miss Jekyll wrote an able illustrated report. . . .'[3]

How much were they each responsible for the success of the collaboration which produced such a contribution to the English way of life—'a Lutyens house with a Jekyll garden'? At this particular stage in their joint career it is possible to refer to at least four reliable sources of information.

First, there is his son, who writes: 'Much has he owed to her

[1] *Life of Sir Edwin Lutyens.*
[2] *The Stranger's Companion in Chester.* Printed for G. Batenham, by J. Fletcher, Bridge St Row, Chester.
[3] *Architecture and Personalities*, by Herbert Baker. Country Life, 1944.

companionship and encouragement; much to her great knowledge of rural tradition. . . . Whilst Miss Jekyll elaborated, with an infallibility of taste and sensitive craftsmanship, the growing feeling for natural and picturesque planting . . . she found in father the ideal interpreter who eventually exalted her limited conception on to the plane of creative formal design.'[1]

Christopher Hussey describes her as Lutyens' fairy godmother. 'That is not quite the right description of Gertrude Jekyll, earthy and practical and determined. Yet fairy godmothers, before now, have issued from woods in no more glamorous guise; and her influence on his character, development, and career during this first decisive decade of his practice was magical.'[2]

Sir Herbert Baker, who did much valuable work in South Africa, and joined forces with Lutyens later in Delhi, wrote of Miss Jekyll: 'She had a great personality and rare gifts . . . but her outstanding possession was the power to see, as a poet, the art and creation of home-making as a whole in relation to Life; the best simple English country life of her day, frugal yet rich in beauty and comfort; in the building and its furnishing and their homely craftsmanship, its garden uniting the house with surrounding nature; all in harmony and breathing the spirit of its creator. She was essentially sane and level-minded in her judgments. . . . This sense of harmony of Art and Life inspired Lutyens in his earlier work in which he so well expressed the best English country life; and it is for this, apart from his work at Delhi, that he will be, I believe, most honoured by posterity.'[3]

The fourth testimony comes from Mr Harold Falkner, himself an architect, and interested especially in the development of Lutyens' work from the first Crooksbury to the addition done ten years later. He remembered well the work going on there, as he was employing the same builder on a job close at hand and said that the first edition of Crooksbury could have been built by anyone. 'It was not a very good house, in fact it was about the average any young architect of the time might have produced. It might even have been built by any good builder of the time without architectural assistance. . . . Ten years later the Chapmans gave L. an opportunity to redeem his former error by the addition of a suite of rooms which nearly masked the original. In these the almost complete Lutyens is revealed—the brickwork and details, the siting of the connecting corridor, the setting out of the

---

[1] *Sir Edwin Lutyens: An Appreciation in Perspective*, by Robert Lutyens. Country Life.
[2] *Life of Sir Edwin Lutyens.*   [3] *Architecture and Personalities.*

32. Miss Ellen Willmott, F.L.S., V.M.H. (1860–1927), author of *The Genus Rosa*.
33. Mrs Theresa Earle (1836–1926), author of *Pot-pourri from a Surrey Garden*.

34. Canon Ellacombe, M.A. (1822–1916), owner of the famous garden at Bitton Vicarage, Gloucestershire, and author of *In a Gloucestershire Garden* and *In My Vicarage Garden*.

35. The Rev. C. Wolley Dod (1826–1904). 'But of all these friendly gardeners, the one whom I felt to be the most valuable was the Rev. C. Wolley Dod, scholar, botanist . . . an enthusiast for plant life, an experienced gardener, and the kindest of instructors.'

36. G. F. Wilson, F.R.S., F.L.S., V.M.H. The garden he created at Wisley now belongs to the Royal Horticultural Society. '. . . I have had the happiness of visiting Mr G. F. Wilson's garden at Wisley, a garden which I take to be about the most instructive it is possible to see.'

37. *Wall and Water Gardens*—'A wood pool best let alone.'

38. *Roses for English Gardens*—'The Garland rose in an old catalpa.'

39. *Old English Household Life*—'A child's cradle of seventeenth-century design found in a cottage.'

garden and paved terrace, garden-walls and courtyards, justified his friends in hailing Lutyens as one of the first architects of the day with the promise of more to come.

'Miss Jekyll had . . . a knowledge of the very finest building practices which she transferred to Lutyens, and that "sense of material" made him different from all other architects of his time. It is interesting to note that in the first Crooksbury he hadn't more than a grain of it but by the time of Little Thakeham and New Place, Shedfield, he fairly oozed with it.'

And so it seems that all the admonitions had borne fruit and the week-ends at Munstead with their leisurely drives round the villages and lanes when 'old houses, farms and cottages were searched for, their modest methods of construction discussed', had sown seeds which had fallen on fertile ground. Mr Oliver Hill recalls being present when some plans were submitted to Miss Jekyll by Lutyens for her approval and criticism (this he did almost up to the end of her life). In this case they were for a large house, perfectly good in every way until a sudden freak idea had flown into his head. 'How were they to get their luggage upstairs? What about an outside lift? Wouldn't that be rather fun?' The answer came smartly, in no uncertain terms: 'Don't be a fool, Ned, don't be a fool!'

There were, of course, other cases where the brake had to be applied. On an expedition to the Isle of Wight, Miss Jekyll had taken him over Mottistone Manor, one of the thoroughbred Stuart homes of England. When, in future, he took his designs for her approval and advice, she would often say, with a twinkle: 'I hope it's modest in manner . . .' (i.e. Mottistone Manor).

He was enthusiastic about the building details of a house or cottage, the materials used, the design and plans, the position and the suitability to its surroundings. She was a gardener and an artist, an expert in colour and in the design of a garden in relation to the house. In *Wall and Water Gardens* she wrote: 'The whole question of the relation of vegetation to architecture is a very large one, and to know what to place where, and when to stop, and when to abstain altogether, requires much knowledge on both sides. . . . The truth appears to be that for the best building and planting . . . the architect and the gardener must have *some* knowledge of each other's business, and each must regard with feelings of kindly reverence the unknown domains of the other's higher knowledge.'[1]

[1] *Wall and Water Gardens*, by Gertrude Jekyll. Country Life, fifth edition, 1913, p. 54.

This shows a respect for architecture and sums up the foundation of the relationship between herself and Edwin Lutyens. But it would have availed nothing if there had not been a deep mutual affection and respect between them. Robert Lutyens wrote: 'The influence of this wise, eccentric and cultivated woman on her generation in general, and on my father in particular, has been on the whole insufficiently acknowledged.'[1]

Another excitement at this time was when Edward Hudson acquired the ruins of Lindisfarne and asked Lutyens to restore the castle. This work went on during 1903–4, and was one of his best restorations. The atmosphere is welcoming with a feeling of solidity, but also of comfort. The wooden doors have large, heavy latches and the gallery—in the style of the Munstead gallery—is an important feature. It is all excellent in workmanship and in design. The garden planting was in Miss Jekyll's charge—and she herself visited the castle a year or two later (*see* letter, p. 107).

During these five years there were three sad losses among her gardening friends. G. F. Wilson of Wisley died on Good Friday, 1902, and the Rev. Wolley Dod and the Dean of Rochester in 1904. G. F. Watts, a painting friend of many years, died in the same year. They were all valued by her, and the Rev. Wolley Dod is especially mentioned by Miss Jekyll in recognition of his help and advice. She describes him as being 'an enthusiast for plant life, an experienced gardener, and the kindest of instructors'. He was seventy-eight and it was reported in *Gardening Illustrated* that 'in later times horticulture has not sustained a more severe loss than in the person of Charles Wolley Dod'. His name lives on in the Wolley Dods rose, a double form of the Apple rose with soft pink flowers.

Also in 1904 there was published (by Longmans) a book of drawings by George S. Elgood entitled *Some English Gardens*, with notes by Gertrude Jekyll. The labour entailed by so much research over a relatively short period of time may be imagined. Of course, her ideas had been forming throughout her life and she wrote entirely from her store of personal knowledge and experience. But the quiet, determined way in which so much work was accomplished can only demand the greatest admiration and respect.

She was now sixty years old. The days of holidays abroad and musical parties were over, although the Blumenthals were still attending evenings where now Percy Grainger played piano pieces, Gervase Elwes sang a group of songs and sometimes Camilla Landi would be the

[1] *Sir Edwin Lutyens: An Appreciation in Perspective.*

star soloist. But Miss Jekyll's energy was reserved for her garden and writing her books and Lady Emily Lutyens recalled that the days had to be carefully regulated to enable her to get through the work. Much of her time was spent out of doors, but when the light became too strong for her eyes this was restricted to a certain number of hours and she had to spend the rest of the day indoors. It was this enforced economy of time which led to her difficulties in showing visitors round the garden, because she knew that seeing her ideas carried out in colour schemes and borders was probably of more value than reading about them, and she was always ready and interested to help, even if they had no knowledge whatever.

She tackled the problem in this way: 'I must ask my kind readers not to take it amiss if I mention here that I cannot undertake to show it [the garden] them on the spot. I am a solitary worker; I am growing old and tired, and suffer from very bad and painful sight.'[1] She still certainly had many visitors of every variety and type, but most of the visits were now made by appointment.

Munstead Wood was, after all, a famous garden. It had been known for some years to the more discriminating members of the gardening world, but since the publication of *Wood and Garden* it was natural that more people should want to come and see for themselves the ideas they had read about, and to get valuable information.

No one took more trouble with someone who showed signs of genuine interest and average intelligence than Gertrude Jekyll, but there were times when her patience was sorely tried. She has recorded with a commendable lightness of touch some of the incidents she experienced in showing people her cherished plantings.

Perhaps the worst of all to bear was the condescending visitor. There was the dreadful case of the squire of rather a large estate who had a reasonably good head gardener. 'My visitor had lately got the idea that he liked hardy flowers, though he had scarcely thrown off the influence of some earlier heresy which taught that they were more or less contemptible—the sort of thing for cottage gardens; still as they were now in fashion, he thought he had better have them. We were passing along my flower-border, just then in one of its best moods of summer beauty, and when its main occupants, three years planted, had come to their full strength, when, speaking of a large flower-border he had lately made, he said, "I told my fellow last autumn to get anything he liked, and yet it is perfectly wretched. It is not as if I wanted

[1] *Colour Schemes for the Flower Garden*, by Gertrude Jekyll. Country Life, third edition, 1914.

anything out of the way; I only want a lot of common things like that", waving a hand airily at my precious border, while scarcely taking the trouble to look at it.'[1]

There was another visitor with just about the same level of 'appreciative insight, who, contemplating some cherished garden picture, the consummation of some long-hoped-for wish, the crowning joy of years of labour, said: "Now, look at that; it is just right, and yet it is quite simple—there is absolutely nothing in it; now, why can't my man give me that?" '[2]

Such insensitivity seems almost incredible, but these are recorded incidents reported from Miss Jekyll's own experiences. So many people refused to believe that any trouble had been taken to produce effects. They would give the credit to luck, to the soil, or to green fingers; as Miss Jekyll reports—'to anything rather than to the plain fact that I love it well enough to give it plenty of care and labour. They assume a tone of complimentary banter, kindly meant no doubt, but to me rather distasteful, to this effect: "Yes, of course it will grow for you; anything will grow for you; you have only to look at a thing and it will grow." I have to pump up a laboured smile and accept the remark with what grace I can, as a necessary civility to the stranger that is within my gates, but it seems to me evident that those who say these things do not understand the love of a garden.'[3] She found 'gush' particularly difficult to deal with.

Miss Jekyll reports with delight the effect on some visitors of her attempts at artificial rock-making. 'The wood path . . . begins at another point of the small lawn next the house, and passes first by a turf walk through a mounded region of small shrubs and carefully placed pieces of the local sandstone. Andromeda, skimmia and alpenrose have grown into solid masses, so that the rocky ridges peer out only here and there. And when my friends say, "But then, what a chance you had with that shelf of rock coming naturally out of the ground," I feel the glowing warmth of an inward smile and think that perhaps the stones have not been so badly placed.'[4]

Then there was the case of the young undergraduate, perhaps hoping to show off a little, making the suggestion that it might be possible to alter the colour of flowers by treating their roots with strong chemicals. The reply was given quietly in the negative, and was followed—it is reported[5]—by a very long and embarrassing silence.

There was a difficult occasion for Mr Falkner, when he was employed

[1] *Wood and Garden*, p. 277.   [2] Ibid., p. 278.   [3] Ibid., p. 141.
[4] *Colour Schemes for the Flower Garden*, p. 20.   [5] L. Pearsall Smith.

40. Miss Jekyll's Boots.

41. Pergola at
Deanery Garden,
Sonning (aga-
panthus in tubs).

42. Folly Farm, Sulhamp-
stead, Berkshire.

43. Millmead, Bramley.
'The ground is a little more
than half an acre, seventy-
seven feet wide and some-
thing over four hundred
feet deep. . . .' 'I do not envy the owners of very large
gardens. The garden should
fit its master or his tastes,
just as his clothes do; it
should be neither too large
nor too small, but just comfortable.'

44. Part of the Pergola at
Hestercombe, Somerset.

to turn away an unauthorised visitor who, unknown to him, was a close relative. Mr Falkner said: 'G.J. was amused, but neither the visitor nor I were.' He was one of her most regular visitors and describes being summoned by a postcard on a certain day at a certain time every month; although this went on over a period of twenty years, he always had to wait for the necessary passport of the postcard. He recalls his first visit, arriving by bicycle up the long hill from Godalming. It was a hot day when even the handlebars of his bicycle were hot to hold, and his straw boater, high stiff collar and Norfolk jacket worn with tapered knickerbockers did little to alleviate the heat.

After many years of visits Mr Falkner felt that he might be allowed to introduce a friend, which he did on one or two occasions, 'with varying results'. One was the secretary of the R.H.S., and this visit had an object as it was hoped that something might be arranged, through the auspices of the R.H.S., to preserve the Munstead garden as a memorial after her death. 'But turn the conversation as I would, it could not be got into the groove. The secretary had been prompted and did his best. We talked of future developments of the R.H.S., preservation of gardens, the importance of design, even colour in the garden (a very favourite subject), but the future of Munstead Wood was evidently not to be discussed, and it may only have been a coincidence but it was two months before I received my next postcard to "come again".'

Visitors were, on the whole, kept in watertight compartments, but one could expect to meet anyone walking round the garden, from a local amateur to a cabinet minister; Mr Falkner remarks that 'they would all get the same treatment'.

Mr Cowley was also a regular visitor over many years, and as he came from a distance, used to spend the night either at Munstead Wood, or with Sir Herbert Jekyll at Munstead House. The pony and trap was sent to meet him at Godalming station—'I'll send the sheltie for you,' Miss Jekyll would say (meaning the shetland pony). Mr Cowley was known as 'the mystery man', owing to Miss Jekyll's habit of seeing her visitors apart from each other, and was greeted as such on one of his sojourns in Munstead House by someone who had been longing for years to make his acquaintance, but had only so far succeeded in hearing of him.

Mr Oliver Hill recounts a story about the first visit to the Munstead Wood garden of Mr and Mrs Barnes-Brand. Mrs Barnes-Brand (the actress, Amy Brandon-Thomas, whose father wrote *Charley's Aunt*) was young and pretty, without any knowledge of gardening, but soon after her marriage had acquired an old mill with some acres of land. The Barnes-Brands knew that Oliver Hill was a friend of Miss Jekyll and begged him to give them an introduction to her garden. He hesitated for some time, knowing their ignorance of gardening matters, but was finally persuaded, if they would think up some intelligent question to ask Miss Jekyll. He knew she would be glad to explain any query if it was a genuine one. Mr Barnes-Brand thought of a question, but it was not quite the kind of question that Mr Hill had meant. However, he decided to take a chance on it and introduce them. The question was: 'Do frogs make good mothers?'

They were received with great courtesy and not the smallest trace of condescension, though at this stage in her life Miss Jekyll's knowledge was valued by experts all over the country, and these two hardly knew the difference between a nasturtium and a tulip. Mrs Barnes-Brand recalls the first part of their conversation, when her comment on the garden was: 'How gay and exhilarating!' Miss Jekyll was delighted: 'I'm so glad, that's just the effect that I've wanted'. Then, explaining the colour border to them, she went on: 'You start from the cool and you get into the warmth.'

This was the first of many happy visits, always with wonderful teas and delicious cakes, although Miss Jekyll herself, it may be remembered, was only allowed a cup of tea with saccharine. 'She always made time to talk and be helpful, and did not make one feel that she wanted one out of the door', Mrs Barnes-Brand went on, 'and one of her nicest characteristics was her generosity about other gardeners. She was modest about herself and her garden—but not stupidly so.'

As a result of this encouragement, Mrs Barnes-Brand became a keen gardener and on a further visit to Munstead, when she was able to discuss gardening matters with greater confidence, she asked: 'What on earth am I to do—I've got a bog all round the stream?' Miss Jekyll's reply came without hesitation, 'Go down on your knees and thank God for the bog'. The one certain thing that came out of these visits was Miss Jekyll's obvious respect for a happy marriage. They were talking with her one day about how much she contrived to get done. 'How do you manage to do so much?' Mrs Barnes-Brand said. 'By not going to tea-parties', came the smart reply. 'Well, I don't go to tea-parties', answered Mrs Barnes-Brand, rather on the defensive, 'and I should never have time to do all this.' 'No, but, my dear, you're married, and that's one person's occupation', came the much more gentle answer.

There is one particular conversation that Miss Jekyll had when showing a friend round her garden which illuminates her work with the warm glow of her philosophy of life. Her visitor was Mr Logan Pearsall Smith, known best, perhaps, as author of *Trivia* and *More Trivia*. He writes: 'Walking with Miss Jekyll . . . amid the gardens she had created, I had asked her if she really enjoyed it all. "It's difficult", I said, "to possess one's own possessions; in everything that I make or write I see the faults and imperfections; they irritate, they annoy me".

' "I know what you mean," Miss Jekyll answered. "When I come out here I see what's wrong; I get cross about it—it's my own fault sometimes, sometimes the gardener's. But", she added, "now and then when I am thinking of something else I come round the corner suddenly on the house and garden; I catch it unawares. It seems to me all right; and then I enjoy it—I enjoy it very much, I can tell you." '

'Thus long ago', he continues, writing much later, 'what is to me—what has always been—the great perplexity of our human predicament, had presented itself to Miss Jekyll and myself, and she had suggested the way to what, in our mortal condition, is its only possible solution. For are we not all fated to pursue ideals which seem eternally to elude us . . . can we ever escape the jarring contrast between what Ought-to-Be, what Might-be, and what actually Is? And yet, as our philosopher points out wisely, this pursuit of the Ideal is what alone gives a meaning to our existence . . . we catch it, as Miss Jekyll, coming round the corner, sometimes caught it. . . .'[1]

[1] *Reperusals and Recollections,* by Logan Pearsall Smith. Constable, 1937.

CHAPTER IX

1905–1908

Millmead—Design for a small garden—Cottage gardens—
Munstead bunch primroses—Publication of Flower
Decoration in the House *and*
Children and Gardens

Country Life offices (1905), Folly Farm (1905–6 and 1912), Hestercombe (1905) were three of the big architectural successes at this time, and as far as Miss Jekyll was concerned, especially the gardens of Folly Farm and Hestercombe. Another piece of work for which she was responsible was the designing and planning of the grounds for the King Edward Sanatorium at Midhurst for patients suffering from consumption.

Miss Jekyll was finding frequent journeys too tiring by now, and so the plans were worked out on paper to a large extent. The plants were sent in sections with detailed planting instructions for the gardeners. King Edward was greatly interested in these gardens and often went down to Midhurst to see how things were getting on. Miss Jekyll was able to be present at the opening ceremony in June, 1906, when she was congratulated by him 'on the success of her work'. Suffering from a degree of ill-health herself owing to the trouble with her eyes, she was especially glad to be able to design gardens which, by providing light and interesting work for the patients, would keep them out in the air as much as possible and so help their recovery.

But there was still another project—an exciting one—in her mind.

A small piece of unused land close to Bramley—where cottages had been pulled down—came into the market. A year or so earlier Miss Jekyll had walked over it and examined its possibilities, which were considerably enhanced for her by the fact that the view overlooked her old home and the woods where, as a child, she had gone to look for primroses. It was also within sound of the working water-mill. The land was bought so that a house should be built on it 'that should not only be worthy of the pretty site but that should also be the best small house in the whole neighbourhood, both for architectural merit and for convenience and comfort. The ground is a little more than half an acre, seventy-seven feet wide and something over four hundred feet deep, on a rather steep slope facing south-south-east.'[1]

This is one of the most important examples which prove that, in the whole of Miss Jekyll's career, her heart and interest were not in the large estates with sweeping parklands, but in the small domestic gardens of England which lie within the reach of so many garden lovers. As Mr Falkner said: 'She naturally liked doing big gardens—they paid better, and she was always hard up . . . but it was to the struggling small gardener she appealed.'

The architect for the house was, of course, Ned Lutyens and the garden was designed and planted by Miss Jekyll. It was called Millmead and in the first chapter of a book published later and written with Lawrence Weaver called *Gardens for Small Country Houses*, Miss Jekyll writes about it. The garden is described in loving detail with many illustrations of plans and photographs. Mr Falkner, previously a devotee of the 'formal' garden, pays to it this tribute: 'More or less by accident I saw the garden of Millmead, at Bramley. It was June. I had been accustomed to gardens which were only just beginning to promise in June. I was struck "all of a heap". I have never seen anything before, nor since, as perfectly developed, so exquisite in every detail, so much in so small a space. Weaver and G.J. subsequently wrote a detailed account of the whole plan . . . a very worthy and painstaking account, but it was as nothing to the effect on me.

'In colour, texture, form, background, setting, smell and association —time of day about six on a June evening—it was perfect. It was to me the work of a fairy or wizard, and I had found it right under my own nose within a few hundred yards of the house in which I was born, but till then absolutely unknown to me. Since then I have come to know its author more intimately than any other colleague. I have seen many of the great gardens in this country and I have never had the least inclination to alter this opinion. (By the word "association" I mean that it was English—typical of the English village; owing something perhaps to a hundred foreign influences, but having so absorbed them that their origin is lost and they have become our own.)'

This is so frequently the kind and size of garden which has to be dealt with that it is encouraging to find that it is the one selected

[1] *Gardens for Small Country Houses*, by Gertrude Jekyll and Sir Lawrence Weaver. Country Life, 1912, p. 1.

by Miss Jekyll when she had a free choice. 'The size of a garden has very little to do with its merit', she writes. 'It is merely an accident relating to the circumstances of the owner. It is the size of his heart and brain and goodwill that will make his garden either delightful or dull, as the case may be, and either leave it at the usual monotonous dead-level, or raise it, in whatever degree may be, towards that of a work of fine art.'[1]

To illustrate her regard for a garden, no matter how small as long as the heart of the owner and his 'brain and goodwill' are in it, there is the story of the Lancashire factory boy who wanted advice for his window-box, already mentioned in Chapter IV. It is hardly necessary to say that advice was sent—and, knowing Miss Jekyll, one feels sure that as much care and thought went into it as into the plans for Munstead or Renishaw.

Miss Jekyll goes on to describe the enthusiastic letters she received from the boy, full of interest and questions, and how difficult it was to 'restrain him from killing his plants with kindness, in the way of liberal doses of artificial manure'. She concludes: 'The very smallness of the tiny garden made each of its small features the more precious.'[2]

Again, she describes a small garden on the south coast. 'In ordinary hands it would have been a perfectly commonplace thing, with the usual weary mixture. In size it may have been a third of an acre, and it was one of the most interesting and enjoyable gardens.I have ever seen. . . .' She ends her description by saying: 'I am always thankful to have seen this garden, because it showed me, in a way that had never been so clearly brought home to me, how much may be done in a small space.'[3]

But perhaps best of all she loved the cottage gardens, expressing her affection for the flowers which she found in them and her regard for their planting.

'Some of the most delightful of all gardens are the little strips in front of roadside cottages. They have a simple and tender charm that one may look for in vain in gardens of greater pretension. And the old garden flowers seem to know that there they are seen at their best; for where else can one see such wallflowers, or double daisies, or white rose bushes; such clustering masses of perennial peas, or such well-kept flowery edgings of pink, or thrift, or London Pride.'[4] These last-named were some of her favourite flowers, especially the London Pride.

Many of the precious flowers we love and treasure today were, in the

---

[1] *Wood and Garden*, p. 171.   [2] Ibid., p. 186.   [3] Ibid., pp. 171–2.   [4] Ibid., p. 185.

years of Gertrude Jekyll's childhood, only to be found in the cottage gardens, having been turned out of more ostentatious gardens in favour of some new introduction from abroad or half-hardy plants cosseted through the winter in Paxton's greenhouses. These last were the culprits of the bedding-out system, against which William Robinson fought so severe a battle. George Eliot, writing about the time of the late fifties (only five years before *Romola* in which Madame Bodichon was featured), describes the glorious, but orderly, confusion which was the hallmark of these gardens at that time, and the charming abundance of fruit, vegetables and flowers which presented together 'all that was pleasant to the eyes and good for food. The rich flower border . . . had its taller beauties, such as moss and Provence roses, varied with espalier apple trees; the crimson of a carnation was carried out in the lurking crimson of the neighbouring strawberry beds; you gathered a moss rose one moment and a bunch of currants the next; you were in delicious fluctuation between the scent of jasmine and the juice of gooseberries.'[1]

Throughout her writings Gertrude Jekyll acknowledges not only the enchantment of the cottage gardens and her respect for them, but also her debt to them. She expresses her gratitude for small hints or useful ideas to be found there. 'I have learnt much from the little cottage gardens that help to make our English waysides the prettiest in the temperate world. One can hardly go into the smallest cottage garden without learning or observing something new. It may be some two plants growing beautifully together by some happy chance, or a pretty mixed tangle of creepers, or something that one has always thought must have a south wall doing better on an east one.'[2]

The acknowledgment of having 'learnt' something occurs continually in her books. Driving through the Surrey lanes she kept her eyes open to notice what lessons she could. People, by now, were coming or writing from all over the country to ask her advice, but many of her own most valuable hints were picked up from the local people and from their experience in their small gardens. 'Not infrequently in passing along a country road, something is seen that may well serve as a lesson in better planting. The lesson is generally one that teaches greater simplicity—the doing of one thing at a time; the avoidance of overmuch detail.'[3]

There is a special reference to roses: 'A good many years ago I came upon it [Reine Blanche] in a cottage garden in Sussex, and thought I

---

[1] *Scenes of Clerical Life*, by George Eliot.   [2] *Wood and Garden*, p. 4.
[3] *Colour Schemes for the Flower Garden*, p. 115.

had found a white Damask. The white is a creamy white, the outsides of the outer petals are stained with red, first showing clearly in the bud. The scent is delicate and delightful, with a faint suspicion of magnolia. A few years ago this old rose found its way to one of our meetings of the Royal Horticultural Society, where it gained much praise. It was there that I recognised my old friend and learned its name. I am fond of the old *Rosa alba*, both single and double and its daughter, maiden's blush. How seldom one sees these roses except in cottage gardens; but what good taste it shows on the cottager's part. . . . I have also learnt from cottage gardens how pretty are some of the old roses grown as standards . . . I have taken the hint, and have now some big round-headed standards, the heads a yard through, of the lovely Celeste and of Madame Plantier that are worth looking at, though one of them is rather badly shaped this year, for my handsome Jack (donkey) ate one side of it when he was waiting outside the studio door while his cartload of logs was being unloaded.'[1]

One of Miss Jekyll's favourite plants was *Yucca filamentosa*, and it was from a cottage garden that she learnt a valuable secret for helping it through the winter. 'I found it in a cottage garden, where I learnt a useful lesson in protecting plants, namely, the use of thickly-cut peaty sods. The good wife had noticed that the peaty ground of the adjoining common, covered with heath and gorse and mossy grass, resisted frost much better than the garden . . . and it had been her practice for many years to get some thick dry sods with the heath left on and to pack them close round to protect tender plants. In this way she had preserved her fuchsias of greenhouse kinds, and calceolarias and the yucca in question (being rather a tender one).'[2]

Again, of a particularly fine hollyhock—one of a pure pink colour with a wide outer frill—she writes: 'It came first from a cottage garden, and has always since been treasured. I call it pink beauty.'[3]

And, 'I remember another cottage garden that had a porch covered with the golden balls of *Kerria japonica*, and China roses reaching up the greater part of the low walls of half timber and plastering. . . .' There is another example of a wall plant introduced into her own garden on this account. 'In remembrance of the cottage example there is *Pyrus japonica* under the long sitting room window.'[4]

A comment on her love of cottage garden flowers also comes in a conversational piece about her written by E. V. Lucas. 'If one wanted to see in those days the flowers she has taught us to cultivate and honour

[1] *Wood and Garden*, p. 78.   [2] Ibid., pp. 91-92.   [3] Ibid., p. 105.
[4] *Colour Schemes for the Flower Garden*, p. 116.

—the stocks and larkspurs and delphiniums—we had to go to the villages and look at cottage gardens'.[1]

But perhaps the greatest 'find' of all in a cottage garden was the forerunner of the Munstead Bunch primroses. As it is one of the achievements of gardening, it seems important enough to quote fully in her own words from an article which she wrote years later for *The Garden*.

'It must have been quite forty-five years ago, sometime in the early seventies of the last century, that I came upon a bunch-flowered primrose in a cottage garden. I was familiar with the old laced polyanthus, and had seen some large flowered ones of reddish colouring; but one of a pale primrose colour something between that and white— was new to me, and I secured the plant. The next year, from some other source, came a yellowish one, much of the same character. They were of a quality that would now be thought very poor, but they were allowed to seed and, among the seedlings, some of the best were kept.

'Gradually, from yearly selection, the quality improved and, as the grower's judgment became more critical, so more and more of the less satisfactory primroses were discarded. It was an immense pleasure, as the years went on, to see the coming of some new type or some new degree of colouring, and to watch for the strengthening of some desired quality. The strain is kept to whites and yellows only, and though confined within the limits of these colourings, the amount of variation in size, habit, marking and shade of colour is quite remarkable. . . .

'It is these strong yellows and the whites with orange eye that are the showiest; but the ones that personally give me the greatest pleasure are some of those with the more tender tinting. There is one great favourite that I call Lemon Rose; it is of a pure primrose colour, with six wide petals that have handsomely waved edges and a pale lemon blotch; . . . another beauty, called Virginie, is flat and white, with an eye that may be called citron, for it is paler than any lemon colour. . . .

'The primrose garden is in a region where there are a few oak trees and where some additional nuts and hollies have been planted. It has large, continuous beds with narrow paths between. . . . The seed is kept till the spring, when it is sown and the seedlings pricked out into shaded beds or empty frames, to be finally planted out in any suitable weather in the later summer. Some are of the opinion that the seed should be sown as soon as ripe. I have tried both ways and find that the spring sowing is the more suitable in my garden. The soil is naturally a poor sand, but has been gradually enriched by constant working and fresh

[1] *The Barber's Clock*, by E. V. Lucas. Methuen, 1931.

manuring, with cow manure when procurable, before each replanting. The primroses do not seem to mind being in the same place year after year. Drought is a great enemy; a rather unusual degree of success this year I attribute to the good spring rains that came at just the right intervals.'[1]

Another disciple of the cottage garden was William Robinson himself, not only on account of its charm, but of lessons to be learnt from it. 'May their charms never grow less! They often teach lessons that "great" gardeners should learn and are pretty from violet and snowdrop time till the fuchsia bushes bloom nearly into winter.' He goes on: 'Those who look at sea or sky or wood see beauty that no art can show; but among the things made by man nothing is prettier than an English cottage garden.'[2]

In the same year as the Millmead experiment there came the deaths of two friends, one of whom probably meant more to her than any other and to whom she owed most in her knowledge and use of colour. These were Canon Musgrave, who was a near neighbour and whose sister spoke to me in such kindly terms about Miss Jekyll, and the other was 'Brabbie'.

Hercules Brabazon had been a good friend over many years, instructing her in the subject she loved best, with, according to Ruskin, similar talents and ideas to Turner. His death must have been a great sadness to her. If she had contrived and in the end achieved a special colour effect in the garden, she knew that he would have appreciated it and known what she was trying to do. She often thanked him for all he had shown her in the use of colour and gave to him the credit if she found she was able to carry out any of his teaching. He was a gentle, kind man and was recognised as a master of water-colour painting in time for him to realise that he was appreciated. He died on 17th May, 1906, and was buried in Sedlescombe churchyard. The letter opposite was written to Mrs Combe, his sister.

In 1907 came the next publication. To Miss Jekyll it may not have been a landmark. It was not her most important book, but it *is* important today because it was one of the pioneer books on flower arrangement which is now popular and which has developed so much during the last fifty years. Perhaps here was one of the books which helped to shape and encourage the movement on its way.

In her Preface, Miss Jekyll describes flower decoration as 'a branch

[1] *The Garden*, 22nd June, 1918.
[2] *The English Flower Garden*, by William Robinson. Fifth edition, 1896.

The Castle, Holy Island
Northumberland

May 17th ~ MUNSTEAD WOOD, GODALMING

Dear Mrs Combe

With truest sorrow
I hear of my old friend's death.

When old age comes,
with its weakness & weariness,
perhaps one ought not to wish
life to be prolonged; but in the
case of so good a friend of
many years one cannot help
clinging to the mere fact of
life.

Nobody had helped me
more than Mr Boxbagor
to understand and enjoy

the beauty of Colour and
of many matters concerning
the fine arts and I am
always most truly thankful
to have been able to count
him among my friends
truer.
Yrs sincerely
Gertrude Jekyll

Fig. 2

of gardening', perhaps because her own approach to the subject would obviously come through gardening, or perhaps because she realised how important it is to have a knowledge of the methods of producing the flowers and knowing which are the hardy ones and at what time of the year to expect them. It is not enough to know how to arrange flowers, it is also important to have some knowledge of the flower as a whole—its leaves, stem, habitat, germination.

The gardening and the flower arrangement were all based on the same fundamental principles. There were not separate sets of rules for each. 'In garden arrangement, as in all other kinds of decorative work, one has not only to acquire a knowledge of what to do, but also to gain some wisdom in perceiving what it is well to let alone.'[1]

Mr Christmas Humphreys, in his history of Buddhism, says: 'The Japanese have par excellence what the scriptures of Zen in China sometimes advised in vain: a knowledge of where to stop. In their gardens as in their architecture, in the arrangement of flowers as in their dress, the minimum is expressed and the maximum left for the beholder to supply.'

This was Miss Jekyll's touchstone. This was born in her and developed through her training in art and her innate good taste. She did not have to learn from the Japanese, but she was ready to admit a debt to them. She was also, as in her love for the English countryside and the cottage gardens and customs of the English village, aware of the necessity for the flower creation to have an English character so that it would combine with English furnishings. She wanted a simple flower arrangement showing off the flowers in a container suitable to its surroundings and fitting in with the English scene.

There is an excellent chapter on the use of wild flowers for the house, and a most useful one on what flowers to grow and how to preserve them as long as possible when they are cut. She advocates a long, deep drink before arranging, much more than adding drugs and chemicals to the water.

Perhaps the most valuable contribution that Miss Jekyll makes to the art of flower arrangement is her use of colour. She suggests certain flowers being used together as a painter would suggest colours to be used from his paintbox. Her knowledge of which colours to blend together, which colours stand up to the light, and which colours to introduce under certain conditions, e.g. her use of white—these ideas have the greatest value for the student of flower arrangement. Whoever reads these colour suggestions is learning not just from someone who loves

[1] *Wall and Water Gardens*, p. 63.

flowers, and who knows about growing them and how to arrange them; they are learning from an artist, how to paint with colours. One is introduced to the juxtaposition of colours, and has explained how one colour reacts upon another.

Her suggestions when writing about colour are characteristic of her knowledge of her subject. She knows so well the immensity of it, that she is hesitant to make definite statements.

An example of this comes into her chapter of flower arrangement in *Home and Garden*. 'If I may suggest a general rule, I should say, use warm colours (reds and yellows) in harmonies, and cold ones (blues and their allies) in contrasts. But one must be content to be able to suggest in the vaguest way only when writing about colour, except in the case of a flower or substance whose colour is constant, for except by such reference no tint can be accurately described. It is very easy to say pink, but pink covers a wide range, from warm ash-colour to pale salmon red, and from the tint of a newborn mushroom to that of an ancient brick. One might prepare a range of at least thirty tints—and this number could easily be multiplied—all of which might be called pink . . .'[1]

This was the year 1907. There had been the publication of the book on flower arrangement. There were intensive labours going on in the production of the 'Munstead primroses'. A museum had been opened at Guildford Castle by the Surrey Archaeological Society and, during this year, she presented to it the larger part of her collection of local craftsmanship in the domestic arts, including 'a unique series of lighting and cooking utensils'.

In the present Short Guide to Guildford Museum there is the following paragraph relating to Miss Jekyll's bequest:

'Among the many exhibits which illustrate the daily life of the last three or four centuries, pride of place must be given to the well-known Gertrude Jekyll collection. It was in fact the acquisition of this collection by the Surrey Archaeological Society which led directly to the enlargement of the Museum in 1911. In the last decades of the nineteenth century Miss Jekyll rescued from destruction all kinds of household objects, even then rapidly passing out of use, from the cottages and farmsteads of South West Surrey, and her collection of lighting and cooking utensils, jugs and bottles, and so on, is now a valuable source of social history.'

The seventeenth-century cradle, one of the most interesting of these exhibits, came from a cottage. 'Its solid head tells of the need of protection

[1] *Home and Garden*, p. 143.

from draught; it has rockers and handles at both ends'[1] (Plate 39).

During the winter of this year two more books were under way. They were both published in 1908, one of them having been suggested by Lutyens. He felt his family should be brought up from an early age in gardening faith, and, probably to make the task of parents easier, it seemed sensible that a reliable and interesting guide to gardening for children should be written.

Mrs Nathaniel Lloyd, the owner of Great Dixter, recalls that at the age of seven her son, Christopher, now the well-known gardening writer, could walk round the garden with her naming almost every flower correctly. On a visit to Miss Jekyll with the boy at this age, Mrs Lloyd recalls the delight of the great lady gardener to meet the young boy gardener, and the words of her blessing to him: 'Go on with the good work'.

Miss Jekyll's book for children would have been little use, however technically accurate, if it had not been written in the language that children would understand and appreciate. How would she know the approach suitable to a child, how to make it simple without being condescending, interesting without being too involved?

Perhaps her opening sentence is as good an indication as any to show her line of thought. 'Well do I remember the time when I thought there were two kinds of people in the world—children and grown ups —and that the world really belonged to the children.'[2] The book was published in 1908.

Magic, adventure and laughter—these are probably the highlights of all childhood everywhere. There are times, of course, when the make-believe and the magic seem to be carried too far. For example to find the bathroom walls covered with thick gluey material, made up from a mixture of shoe polish, soap flakes, soft sugar and raw eggs can be disturbing, even if it is supposed to create the illusion that one is taking a bath down below the bed of the sea. The addition of clumps of smelly seaweed saved from the summer holidays does nothing to alleviate the situation, especially when the substance is found to have formed a rock-like cement, almost impossible to scrape off.

To enter into the spirit of such an adventure from an adult's point of view can hardly be expected, but it is particularly rewarding to be thought worthy of inclusion in some lesser experiments of make-believe or adventure.

[1] Described in *Old English Household Life*, p. 67, by Gertrude Jekyll. Batsford, 1925. (Revised and enlarged edition of *Old West Surrey*, pub. Country Life, 1904.)
[2] *Children and Gardens*, p. 10.

Miss Jekyll's capacity for entering into the world of a child was one of her greatest accomplishments. Bernard Darwin, in an appreciative Introduction to her book written for children, pays her the following tribute: 'She will always be remembered as a great gardener, but she deserves to be equally well remembered as a great writer for children. She has the two essential qualities, first a perfect seriousness, second a feeling for what I should be inclined to call romance if I did not think that she would have deemed it an affected word; she would rather have called it adventure. The first of these qualities could not be better illustrated than by her title of her book *Children and Gardens*. It is so entirely simple and clear, almost bald. So many people would have wanted a title that should be consciously pretty or fanciful. It is easy to imagine dreadful ones such as "How does your garden grow?" *Children and Gardens* says in the fewest possible words exactly what the book is about. And the whole book is pervaded by this gravity and straight-forwardness. . . . She must have been an ideal playfellow for children because she would not consciously have been playing at all. When she writes that "nothing is so delightful as any sort of playing with water" we feel sure that she means precisely what she says and that she is think-ing at least as much of her own delight as of anybody else's, whether in intellectual contriving or physical splashing.'

There are constant references throughout the book to humour, adventure and magic. Discussing the making of an enormous cowslip ball for May-day, she says: 'The whole thing was most amusing, but then it is always the greatest fun to invent and contrive and get over difficulties.' Then there are the joys of sticky mud. 'It was a grand place for wild flowers', she writes 'and there was a shallow river to paddle in, and heavenly places for paddling where there was mud like thick chocolate'. Giving the first outline of botany she says: 'Of course botany books in general are apt to be dull and dry and alarming. They frighten one by calling things names . . . but I do want you to learn my botany, which is amusing, and is quite simple and easy.'[1]

'Amusing' is a word which she used often and evidently enjoyed. 'It is amusing to see one of the small bumble-bees go into a snapdragon flower to get the honey. . . .' Talking of geometry: 'but the rule-of-thumb way is the most amusing. . . .' 'Columbines are such lovely and amusing flowers. . . .'[2]

Then there was the lure of 'adventure' and 'messing about' and 'make-believe'. 'Perhaps you will say that the lawn is not the sort of place where you expect to meet with adventures,' she wrote. 'Well,

[1] *Children and Gardens*, p. 58.   [2] Ibid. p. 77.

perhaps it is not, and yet such odd and unexpected things happen on it, things that are so deliciously thrilling, that I think I am hardly using too strong a word when I say "adventures". This summer it is hedge-hogs.'[1] One of these adventures with a hedgehog who suddenly appeared on the lawn caused the greatest concern. After Miss Jekyll had photographed him he lay still for so long that she began to fear the worst. But after watching him carefully she noticed a small sign of life when a bluebottle alighted on the corner of one of his eyes. 'I was quite relieved', she wrote, and she went off to the kitchen to get him a sliver of raw mutton. 'Cautiously I approached him and slowly brought the meat close to his nose. He sniffed it, and then at once took-it in his mouth and chumped it up, and seemed to enjoy it immensely. It really was quite an adventure.'[2] (Plate 45.)

Another adventure concerned an owl. 'I must tell you about my owl' she wrote. 'When my house was built eleven years ago I had a little opening left in one of the end gables . . . owls are fond of getting into places of this sort, but though I hoped an owl would come I didn't want to have him flopping about all over our beds at night, and frightening us out of our wits; so just inside the opening I had a wooden enclosure made so that he would have a nice little room to himself. Year after year passed but no owl came. But this spring I saw a dark roundish object lying on the paving just under the opening I had provided for his entrance'. She then went on to describe in careful detail the way that owls produce a pellet. 'They hunt in the late evening and catch and eat numbers of mice, and seem to swallow them whole. Their insides, after digesting the flesh of the mice, work up the fur and bones into long-shaped balls which the owls throw up.' The pellet lying on the paving gave proof that the specially prepared house in the gable was tenanted at last. She summed up the story as 'one of my adventures.[3]'

One day an excitement on the lawn was caused by the appearance of a tortoise. Miss Jekyll did not possess one and could not account for its arrival. 'How it got there I cannot think', she wrote, 'for there are only three houses within a near walk and none of their owners had tortoises. It has always remained an unexplained mystery. But I like mysteries and I hope you do too.'[4]

The style of the writing of this book is friendly and natural—rather like that of someone who is continually delighted and often surprised by the excitements of nature and who is longing to share them with others equally interested. There is a great deal of information—how

---

[1] *Children and Gardens*, p. 18.　　[2] Ibid., p. 83.　　[3] Ibid., p. 86.　　[4] Ibid., p. 83.

45. 'Perhaps you will say that the lawn is not the place where you expect to meet with adventures. Well, perhaps it is not, and yet such odd and unexpected things happen on it . . . that I think I am hardly using too strong a word when I say "adventures". This summer it is hedgehogs.'

46. (Right) Pinkieboy. 'When we meet after an unusual separation of a few hours, as he sees me coming he prepares himself for a good five minutes of pleasant conversation. Its subject is always the same, namely, unqualified admiration and approval of Pinkieboy.'

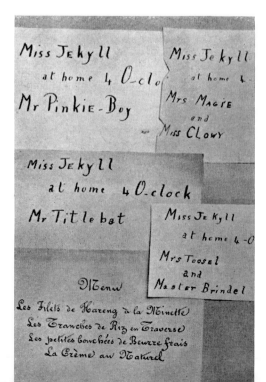

47. 'My youngest niece of nine years old . . . proposed to issue cards of invitation, and said that she would write them herself.'

48 and 49. *Colour Schemes for the Flower Garden.* The Grey Border.

50. The garden at 100, Cheyne Walk, Chelsea, once the home of Sir Hugh Lane. 'Fortunately there existed two fine trees, one a mulberry of noble growth, and these make brave features. A sense of length is given to the garden by the wide parallel stone paths, the middle one of which is interrupted by a round pool.'

to plan a small garden, what to grow in it, things to plant which can be useful for eating, cooking recipes for meals suitable for children to cook themselves, notes on the migration of swallows, useful knots and how to make a camp fire so that it will burn quickly and well and—most important—leaving afterwards no trace of it at all. It is all so unpatronising, giving credit for common sense and ordinary intelligence to her readers: 'but we need not bother about that—you will see what is meant'.

To quote Mr Bernard Darwin again, choosing a typical analogy: 'An old Scottish caddie is said to have reproved a promising but light-hearted young golfer with the words, "No champion was ever freevolous", and it is certain that no great player with children ever permits himself or indeed has any temptation to be so. If the game be one in which there is winning and losing, the good grown-up player may now and then allow himself to be beaten but it is all against the grain, he shrinks almost as sensibly from defeat as from being found out. If the game be one of "pretending", then he pretends with all his might; his playmate may be quite obviously under the table, not even hidden by the tablecloth, but he exclaims, "Where can that tiresome little girl have gone?" with intense conviction. . . .'

Most of us know the situation of meeting one's child, perhaps on the stairs, and of greeting him naturally only to be frowned on fiercely with the words spoken in a hoarse whisper: 'Mum, don't talk to me. I'm *invisible.*' It is no good replying, even with some reason, 'Well, dear, how am I to know?' One is expected to know and that is all there is to it. Miss Jekyll would have understood this situation and treated it with respect. As Mr Darwin says: 'Judging Miss Jekyll purely by this one book we can feel certain that she had in all children's games the unerring instinct for doing the right thing.'

A sad note was struck during this year owing to the death of another old and valued friend. Monsieur Jacques Blumenthal, genial host of the Chalet parties, died on 17th May at his home in Cheyne Walk. He and Madame Blumenthal had moved from 43, Hyde Park Gate, where they had entertained for many years their music-loving friends and it was from the Cheyne Walk address that Monsieur Blumenthal had written on the occasion of Brabazon's death two years earlier. He was laid up at the time having had 'a bad fall from a cab'. Perhaps he never fully recovered from this fall. For Miss Jekyll, to whom these Chalet friendships had meant so much in pleasure, work and a kind of freedom which perhaps she could only feel abroad, another link was gone.

CHAPTER X

1908

Publication of Colour in the Flower Garden

Later editions entitled *Colour Schemes for the Flower Garden* to which
all page numbers in this chapter refer.

'She differed from all other gardeners in the fact that she was an
artist. Gardening was not a craft or even a science to her—it was an
art.' Mr Falkner's comment sends one thinking back some forty or fifty
years to the time of Gertrude Jekyll's art training. The days spent as an
art student and the painting accomplished later, until her eyes troubled
her too greatly, were now going to bear fruit in the book which she also
published in 1908—*Colour in the Flower Garden* (subsequent editions
entitled *Colour Schemes for the Flower Garden*).

This book, as far as it is possible to judge at this distance of time, is
her great contribution to English gardening. Her ideas on colour stand
in a class apart.

She was always most willing to allow for individual variety of taste
in a garden. For instance, talking of 'mixed planting', she says: 'I do
not presume to condemn all mixed planting, only stupid and ignorant
mixed planting. It is not given to all people to take their pleasures
alike. . . .'.[1] But in the matter of colour it is different. Her ideas are not
debatable any more than it is possible to debate about the perfection
of the glass in Fairford church or the lines of a Wren building. They are
the fundamental truths which do not change with fashion or mood.
They are classical, as the ideas of Leonardo da Vinci are classical; that
is to say, it is not claimed that they are original. What *is* original is that
they are applied to gardening.

In her own words: 'Planting ground is painting a landscape with

---

[1] *Wood and Garden*, p. 183.

living things; and as I hold that good gardening takes rank within the bounds of the fine arts, so I hold that to plant well needs an artist of no mean capacity. . . . It is not the paint that makes the picture, but the brain and heart and hand of the man who uses it.' This is repeated again and again in her writing. '. . . the trained eye sees what is wanted, and the trained hand does it, both by an acquired instinct. It is painting a picture with living plants.'[1] Again, '. . . it seems to me that the duty we owe to our gardens and to our own bettering in our gardens is so to use the plants that they shall form beautiful pictures.'

Her reputation as a gardener could, of course, stand on *Wood and Garden* and *Home and Garden*, on *Wall and Water Gardens* and on *Roses for English Gardens*. But it is in this book that the essence of her artistic training is collected together, and it is here that she is first an artist and then a gardener.

In her book *Colour Schemes for the Flower Garden*, Miss Jekyll gives extensive and varied combinations and contrasts of colour for all types of gardens. There are many plans which she drew herself, and numerous photographs, many of which she took herself.

It seems best to tabulate these ideas as far as possible so that one can see easily her suggestions for the use of certain colours, or her arrangement of particular plants together or in contrast—all in connection with a garden of an acre or under.

One of her most general ideas about the use of colour is that flowers which bloom at the same time should be arranged wherever possible close to each other. It is better to have a clump of colour at one time of the year and then a space of green to follow, than to have bits of colour dotted about so that there is always something in flower in a particular bed or border of the garden.

The opening paragraph of her Introduction is encouraging because it does not waive the difficulties: 'To plant and maintain a flower border, *with a good scheme for colour*, is by no means the easy thing that is commonly supposed.' Her answer is 'to devote certain borders to certain times of year; each border or garden region to be bright for from one to three months'.

Another general reminder is that 'it takes two or three or even more years' for certain perennials to come to their full strength, and so no border can be expected to look its best for that length of time. In the meantime, it is advisable to make a plan for a long-term period, leaving gaps to allow for development and growth, and filling in between the

---

[1] *Wood and Garden*, p. 212.

plantings with annuals so that there will not be patches of bare soil. Bare earth can be depressing where there should be flowers or foliage, but the decorative value of green, without flowers, is another matter.

Speaking again of the impossibility of continuous colour everywhere in the garden, she also says: '. . . it is even undesirable to have a garden in blossom all over, and groups of flower-beauty are all the more enjoyable for being more or less isolated by stretches of intervening greenery.'

Perhaps since the turn of the century we have become more conscious of green as a colour in this country, and are at last being wedded to the beauty of leaves and stems, away from the glaring flower-heads of the seed packets. '. . . it is doubtful if we like mere brightness in flowers any better than we do in people . . . there is a great deal of beauty . . . if only we do not insist upon flowers and if we are willing to regard green and brown as colours.'[1] Miss Jekyll had this appreciation at a time when a mass of colour was the aim of most gardeners.

It will be noticed that many of her suggestions include the contrast of one kind of plant against another, often a colour, pale or deep, but showing off beside a different backcloth of green. In a painting the background has always been considered of immense importance, showing up the foreground to its best advantage. In these garden ideas, Miss Jekyll is painting pictures and the background is equally important here.

The contrast of a good-shaped green leaf is used as a foil for a white or crimson lily; the backcloth of an evergreen hedge is used to show up a deep pink climbing rose; one shade of clematis is trained up into another: 'the pale green foliage of the deciduous *Magnolia conspicua* showing as a background to the tender blue of a charming pale delphinium'. A Garland rose is guided through and tumbles out of a yew, and in another place in the garden out of a silver holly.

These are the kind of suggestions that are eminently suitable for a small garden, and they are typical of Miss Jekyll's kind of gardening.

It will also be evident that these ideas are for all parts of the garden— some for the border, some for a wall or a north corner, or a rockery, or for shrubs:

1. White tulips coming through a patch of *Stachys lanata* (p. 30). The grey-leaved *Stachys lanata* may seem an ordinary plant worthy of little respect because it is easy to grow and once started spreads with enthusiasm and energy. If looked at individually, the leaves of this plant, silver-grey and velvet, are lovely in shape and colour; it only becomes tiring when planted in careless profusion. The first small grey spires

[1] *The Contemplative Gardener*, by Jason Hill. Faber and Faber, 1940.

shooting up in the spring, interlaced with milk-white tulips produce an almost ethereal effect.

2. Lilies planted among rhododendrons or other shrubs (p. 14). The success of this kind of planting can be clearly seen at Wisley, where the fresh green shoots of various kinds of lilies are showing while the azaleas and rhododendrons are in flower. Later on, when the lilies are opening, the dark, definite leaves of the shrubs provide a background lit up either by their bright colours or their paper-white petals flecked with gold. Miss Jekyll mentions especially using *Lilium auratum*.

3. Nut trees planted at intervals with garlands of *Clematis montana* swinging between them (p. 29). A cob-nut or hazel is a delicious tree to have in a garden, attractive in growth, not too slow, and carrying a decorative harvest in the autumn. Miss Jekyll draws a plan with four trees spaced fairly well out and from one tree to another a length of rope is hung, along which is trained a *Clematis montana*. This produces the effect of white garlands.

4. For a north wall: a guelder rose with *Clematis montana* (p. 53). It may not be generally known that the guelder rose is quite happy without much sun. The *montana* and the guelder rose flower at about the same time, and grown into each other they provide an interesting juxtaposition of growth which makes for a happy marriage of the two: the more formal leaves and rather abrupt shape of stem and globe-like flower of the guelder rose contrast with the fairylike quality of the *Clematis montana* and its seemingly airborne branches covered with starlike flowers.

5. Paeonies with lent hellebores (p. 36). This is an idea which, while making a good garden picture, seems to have originated in Miss Jekyll's mind from the fact that both plants like the same kind of condition, and why not put them together? This is a point that one is sometimes liable to overlook. Paeonies and hellebores are both rich feeders. They like a deeply prepared ground, shelter, and liberal helpings of manure. The final result is that the hellebores, growing lower than the paeonies, provide a 'picture frame' against which the paeony flowers show up well.

6. Holly, laced with either wild honeysuckle, the Garland rose or a clematis (p. 95). Here is the use of an evergreen tree to show off a climber, either white or pale pink or yellow. A holly comes into its own in the winter months, but during the summer it can be lightened by having something brightly coloured tumbling down amongst the dark leaves.

7. Colour-grouping suggestions for azaleas, rhododendrons and

paeonies (pp. 13–30). (Since Miss Jekyll's day the many new introductions make it difficult to include specific ones. As on p. 13 she refers to *Wood and Garden* where 'some details of this planting were given at length,' her general ideas on their colour grouping are taken from there).

(*a*) *Azaleas*. Miss Jekyll recommends the planting of white azaleas 'at the lower and more shady end of the group', with pale pinks and soft yellows next to the white, building up to the deepest crimson, flame, orange and burnt-orange colours with, if there is still space, a further planting of yellow again.

(*b*) *Rhododendrons*. There are a few notes given about the actual selection and planting. First of all, of course, the individual bushes must be planted well and at great enough distance from each other to avoid overcrowding; the colour must be grouped in harmonies: and it is of the greatest importance to select good varieties beautiful in themselves.

1. Dark crimson and clarets with true pink
2. Light scarlet inclining to rose and scarlet
3. Rose colours merging into deep red
4. Deep red and magenta
5. Crimson or deep wine purples
6. Clear purples and mauves

These six suggestions are made for fairly extensive planting. It is easy enough to select the colour group preferred or most suitable to neighbouring plants and shrubs for a small garden. Miss Jekyll herself had only room for three of the above groups.

(*c*) *Paeonies*. These are divided into three groups, as follows:

1. Tree paeonies—shrubby, flowering in May
2. Chinese paeonies—herbaceous, flowering in June
3. Old garden paeonies—herbaceous

Of tree paeonies, Miss Jekyll particularly mentions the Reine Elisabeth, salmon-rose, with handsome foliage, and the white Bijou de Chusan. Like all tree paeonies these have very fine leaves of an almost dull copper colour shot with blue, and Miss Jekyll describes it as 'sometimes of a metallic quality that faintly recalls some of the variously coloured alloys of metal that the Japanese bronze workers make and use. . . .'

Among the Chinese paeonies and the herbaceous ones there are a number with 'pink or rose-crimson colouring of a decidedly rank quality' and Miss Jekyll advises a careful selection being made so that these may be avoided. She gives a long list of her own favourites, a special one being *Paeonia wittmanniana*, pale yellow (not reliable).

8. For the use of iris and lupin in a June border see Plan I and Plate II of this border at Munstead. For a rock garden in June (p. 50). Small pink pompon roses 'Pompon de Paris' with pale mauve pansies and *Achillea umbellata*, or Rose mignonette with catmint and *Stachys lanata* and *Cineraria maritima*. For a bold effect, a deep strain of the red valerian is suggested with dark scarlet snapdragons.

9. For a border in July (pp. 61–67).

(*a*) Grey at each end—*Stachys lanata*, *Cineraria maritima*, sea-kale, lyme-grass (*Elymus avenarus*), yucca, rue and *Clematis recta*, with, next to them, flowers of clear blue, grey blue, pale yellow and pink, and then, working towards the centre, strong oranges and reds link together with stronger yellows.

(*b*) Gypsophila to follow oriental poppies, to be followed in turn by trailing nasturtiums which will cover over the patches of gypsophila when it has gone brown.

(*c*) White everlasting pea planted behind delphiniums and *Clematis jackmanii* behind the pea. When the stalks of the delphiniums become bare and the foliage turns yellow the everlasting pea is trained over delphinium stalks which are cut short. The clematis is brought over to take the place of the pea in the middle of August when it has finished flowering.

(*d*) Blue and grey. *Delphinium belladonna*—very pure blue—double *Delphinium grandiflorum*, Cape daisy (*Agathaea coelestis*) and *Salvia patens*, white lavender and *Artemisia stelleriana*.

(*e*) Yellow and white. *Verbascum phlomoides*, golden privet, rue, double meadowsweet, and white and pale yellow tall snapdragons.

(*f*) Blue-grey-yellow. *Eryngium oliverianum*, pale and dark spiderworts, *Thalictrum flavum*, *Coreopsis lanceolata*, *Achillea eupatorium* and yellow cannas.

(*g*) Orange-crimson-red. Bergamot, orange lilies, gazanias, scarlet salvia, lychnis and pure scarlet dwarf tropaeolums.

(*h*) Grey-blues, whites, pale yellows. Eryngium, white everlasting pea, calceolaria, yuccas, stachys, santolina, *Cineraria maritima* and sea-kale. Behind this group there is a purple clematis and tall plants of *Verbascum phlomoides*. A spreading bush of *Clematis recta* foliage —the flowers are over—occurs between the purple clematis and the santolina. This foliage is of a 'leaden sort of blueness' and provides an artist's touch to this grey-blue colour scheme.

10. Colour ideas for the border in August.

(*a*) White everlasting pea trained forward over the delphinium stalks as mentioned for July, against a bush of golden privet which is, again, planted against a clump of eulalia (miscanthus) (Japanese striped grass about seven feet height) with tall yellow and white snapdragons.

(*b*) A palest yellow dahlia flushed with pink with, in front, a palest pink penstemon and patches of pale blue spiderwort: then, quite to the front, interspersed among grey foliage, 'cobalt blue' lobelia, a taller lobelia, *Lobelia tenuior*, and blue-flowered Cape daisy.

(*c*) Santolina as a border, backed by lyme-grass.

(*d*) At the back of the border a perennial sunflower, then *Achillea eupatorium* (*A. Silipendulina*), and in front of this, again, a wide-spreading group of *Eryngium oliverianum*. The point of the sunflower is that when the achillea and the eryngium are nearly over the sunflower is pulled down and forward over them, when it will send up flower stalks growing upwards from the horizontal stems, resulting in a sheet of bloom in September.

(*e*) Deep red hollyhocks towering at the back of the border close to red, scarlet and orange dahlias, leading on to scarlet penstemons, African marigolds, scarlet gladiolus, and the dwarf brilliant scarlet salvia, *Helenium pumilum*, and scarlet and orange dwarf nasturtium at the front.

(*g*) *Gypsophila paniculata* forming 'cloudy masses' at intervals amongst the brilliant colours, which, introduced in this way, has 'considerable pictorial value'. The 'cloudy masses' have the same effect as funkia (hosta) or megasea (bergenia) foliage—that is, they show up the bright colours of the flowers of this part of the border and, in fact, provide the light and shade so essential to the successful showing off of colour.

(*h*) Dahlias and hollyhocks at the back of the border in pale yellow and white, and in front of them, *Saponaria officinalis* and pale pink penstemon.

(*i*) Near the path, to the front of the border, *Stachys lanata*, *Cineraria maritima*, *Artemisia stelleriana*, catmint with, behind them, godetia Double Rose, white snapdragons and *Lilium longiflorum*, planted between bushes of lavender and gypsophila.

(*j*) To the back of the border again, and behind the foregoing gronps, white achillea, The Pearl is planted, together with globe-thistle and silver thistle (*Eryngium giganteum*). At the back of these there are pink hollyhocks.

11. Gardens of special colourings.

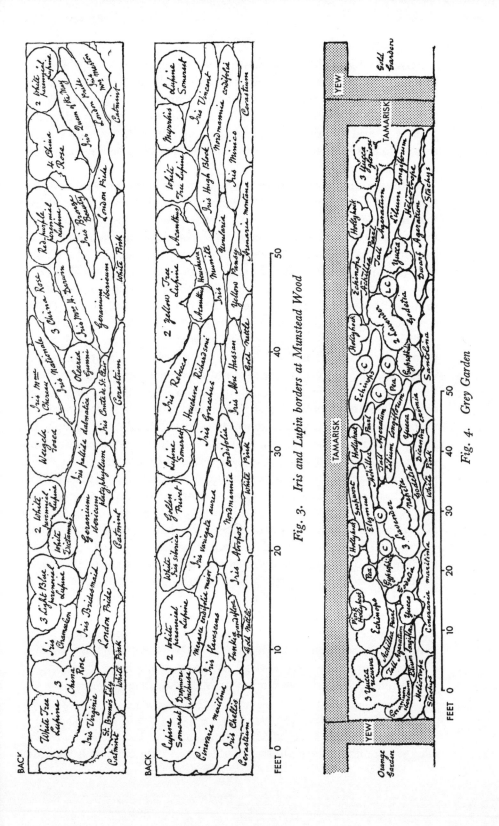

Fig. 3. *Iris and Lupin borders at Munstead Wood*

Fig. 4. *Grey Garden*

Miss Jekyll gives ideas for planting in colour groups of shades of one colour; grey, gold, blue, etc. People with small gardens may have the immediate reaction that this is not for them. But it is surprising, as I think it will be found, what can be done in small space with colour grouping, and it can be interesting and exciting to try out some of these schemes, and to have a grey corner or a blue bed even in quite a small garden.

At Sissinghurst Castle there is a well-known grey-and-white garden, shut off from the main part of the whole by a wall on one side and by a sizeable hedge. This garden is again divided into smallish beds bordered by low box hedges. Any of these beds could be incorporated into a garden of less than an acre, or half an acre, without the whole effect of the colouring being lost. It can be done in quite a small way by devoting one end of the border to a certain colour scheme, but if it is shut off from other beds by a small hedge or even only separated by a grass verge it is likely to have a more complete effect (Plate 58).

Perhaps the most important thing to remember when working with plants of one colour is that there is the problem of light and shade, which may be more obvious in painting than in any other medium. For example, there is the painting by Renoir of the Ile de Paris, which, at some distance, looks almost completely 'blue'. It is only on closer examination that it is seen to contain little actual 'blue' paint, but plenty of ultramarine, vandyk brown, deep purple, grey, crimson, off-white and burnt sienna. Miss Jekyll comments on this use of one colour painted in against another to bring out an effect (p. 98). 'It is a curious thing that people will sometimes spoil some garden project for the sake of a word. For instance, a blue garden, for beauty's sake, may be hungering for a group of white lilies or for something of palest lemon-yellow, but it is not allowed to have it because it is called the blue garden, and there must be no flowers in it but blue flowers. . . . Surely the business of the blue garden is to be beautiful as well as to be blue. My own idea is that it should be beautiful first, and then just as blue as may be consistent with its best possible beauty. Moreover, any experienced colourist knows that the blues will be more telling—more purely blue—by the juxtaposition of rightly placed complementary colour.'

Here follow suggestions: (Miss Jekyll must, many times, have applied these same ideas in the medium of paint on a canvas).

The grey garden (p. 99, Plan II).

The grey garden is so called because most of the plants have grey foliage—the flowers are white, pale lilac and pale pink. It is a garden planned for August, because that is the time when these plants which are suitable in colour are at their best. At Sissinghurst, Miss Sackville-West planted soft yellow verbascum and pale pink Japanese anemones in her grey garden, with many white flowers.

The hedge forming the background of the grey garden is of feathery-leaved tamarisk (*Tamarix gallica*). Against the hedge are hollyhocks —Miss Jekyll mentions 'pink beauty'—and one can imagine sulphur yellow and white also making a useful mixture. White everlasting pea, echinops and the pale pink double soapwort are also planted towards the back of the border. Then come clumps of yucca, achillea The Pearl, gypsophila, lavender and the blue-green lyme grass, elymus. In between these are groups of *Lilium longiforum* and *Lilium candidum*. Along the front of the border come clumps of *Stachys lanata*, santolina, nepeta, white pinks, *Cineraria maritima* with, close behind them, godetia and *Ageratum mexicanum*, a plant or two of heliotrope and of *Geranium ibericum*. Miss Jekyll also includes purple clematis of the Jackmanii class which is planted so that it can be trained over the clumps of gypsophila when they have flowered and are over, as was done in the mixed border.

After such a list one needs to recover one's breath. Obviously there are enough plants here to fill a fair-sized border, and the very mention of them presents a glamorous picture of what possibilities there are. But a grey garden can still be painted with less material, and such generous suggestions may be drawn upon to suit one's purse and the number of square feet of flower bed available. Miss Jekyll herself was not able to indulge in all of these colour gardens and concentrated chiefly on a grey border (see p. 98) but she enjoyed working out the plans for different ones, which are to be found in detail in her book.

To make the best of a small space needs even greater ingenuity than having unlimited opportunity. Mistakes show up more than in a big border and the wrong juxtaposition of colour or shape is more obvious. And so these suggestions come almost in the nature of a challenge to experiment to see what can be achieved.

The gold garden (p. 109, Plan III).

Miss Jekyll plans the gold garden next to the grey, to give a feeling of sunlight and warmth after the cool effect of the other. (She does, in fact, arrange for the grey garden to be between the gold and the orange, to give this suggestion of warmth on either side of it.) The use of the word 'gold' may be misleading. Perhaps the word 'yellow' should be substituted. She comments on this point: 'the word "gold" in itself

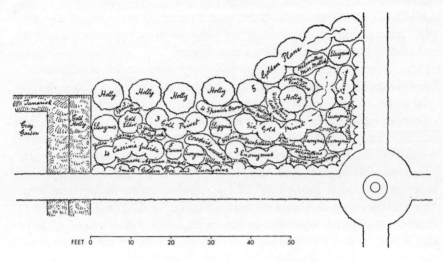

Fig. 5. A Corner of the Gold Garden

is, of course, an absurdity; no growing leaf or flower has the least resemblance to the colour of gold'. She qualifies this by explaining that the word 'gold' has now acquired a meaning which covers and enlarges on the word 'yellow'. However, 'gold' or 'yellow', the flowers to be planted are much the same.

For the background of this garden Miss Jekyll suggests a free planting of gold holly and the golden plane tree, controlled by cutting so that it is kept within reasonable limits. As the plane trees are, of course, deciduous, she recommends that there should be a line of gold yews and one or two more variegated hollies to help along the effect during the winter.

A small, low-clipped hedge of gold-variegated box is to be the front of the border, or gold-variegated euonymus trimmed down to about two feet. At the front, inside the hedge, are to be planted the yellow African marigold—on no account the orange—and yellow snapdragons, *Iris ochroleuca*, coreopsis, euonymus and a pale helianthus such as *laetiflorus*. Behind these come yellow hollyhocks, Spanish broom, bushes of golden privet, clumps of evening primrose and verbascum. (It gives me great pleasure to be able to include the golden privet in this list. Habitually despised, or ill-treated by tight, formal cutting, it can have the effect of a splash of sunlight if allowed to grow freely into a natural shape and develop long, spreading branches. With its clear-cut yellow leaves it can provide an excellent contrast if rightly placed among dark-leafed shrubs. Miss Jekyll defends the golden privet, and it is mentioned farther on in this chapter when she deals with the use of what are described as 'common' plants.)

The gold garden, by nature of the plants in it, is largely dependent on its shrubs and hedges. Miss Jekyll gives a timely note of warning about the temptation to interpret exactly the word 'gold' in order to bring into it still further variety. One pitfall is the word 'goldfish' and she stresses that the colour of goldfish is so far from the soft yellow-gold of this garden that, even if there is a pond or small water garden or tank, it must not be filled with goldfish. The harsh orange of the fish, though quite beautiful in itself, would be quite wrong and utterly out of place. Another trap into which it might be easy to fall could be a sundial with incised gold lettering. Again, both the texture and the colour of the gilding would be wrong.

'Never', writes Miss Jekyll, 'hurt the garden for the sake of the tempting word.'

This is how an artist has to think of his colours when painting a picture, and no point is too fine for him to consider.

The blue garden (p. 112).

Miss Jekyll plans the blue garden to follow on next to the yellow. She will not allow any purple-blues here, only pure blue, with white and palest yellow. This is, of course, owing to the proximity of the gold garden where mauve-blues would make an unfortunate contrast. There are so many suggestions for this garden that the difficulties of selection must be difficult, largely because to produce a blue garden Miss Jekyll uses many other colours than blue. It is as if one were presented with a box of water colours and brushes and a canvas and given the opportunity to use almost all the colours.

The background for this garden is of yew, producing a grand screen of dark green to show up the various tones and shades to their best advantage. Against the hedge are plantings of white and perennial lupins, delphiniums, tall yellow thalictrum, white hollyhocks, anchusa and *Clematis recta*. The Japanese grass, eulalia (*Miscanthus sinensis variegatus*), tall and white-striped, also planted against the hedge behind the groups of delphiniums, looks well with the maize. Rue, eryngium, white snapdragons, palest yellow snapdragons, *Salvia patens*, *Spiraea aruncus* (*A. sylvester*), *Lilium longiflorum* and *Lilium candidum* all come in the middle of the border with *Delphinium grandiflorum*, *Delphinium belladonna*, agathaea, yucca and clematis. At the front of the blue border come plantings of foliage plants—*Funkia sieboldii* (*Hosta*

Fortunei) and *F. grandiflora* (*H. plantaginea*), with variegated coltsfoot, lithospermum and phacelia.

The blueish foliage of the rue, yucca and clematis recta play just as important a part in this blue garden as the blue of the flowers.

The green garden (p. 113)

Naturally, the green garden depends to a large extent on use and contrast of shape, texture and colour of foliage. There are flowers, and they are nearly all white.

Green aucubas, skimmias and *Ruscus racemosus* (*Danaë racemosa*) are contrasted with the foliage of acanthus, hosta, *Iris foetidissima*, and *Lilium candidum* and *Lilium longiflorum* provide some of the flowers. White tulips, *Helleborus olympicus*, *Paeonia whitleyi*, and white snapdragons and foxgloves give some flowering at different times of the year.

The orange garden (plan, p. 102)

This is the smallest on Miss Jekyll's plan, perhaps because a little of this colour goes a long way. It is planted with Rudbeckia golden glow, double helianthus and red-hot pokers. Then come groups of gladioli in orange and yellow, orange African marigold, *Lychnis chalcedonica*, coreopsis, achillea (yellow), *Salvia splendens*, helenium and *Lilium croceum*.

These are some of Miss Jekyll's suggestions for colour gardens or colour groupings in a border or for small separate flower beds— whichever is most suitable to one's own garden. They can be adapted, either supplemented or minimised, to any particular requirement. The important thing is that the fundamentals are there—the right selection of colour and shape—and they are the result of careful thought and experiment. Some of these ideas were tried out in the garden of Munstead Wood over a period of thirty years. This in itself is almost unique. Miss Jekyll describes herself as an amateur, but few amateurs have the opportunity or the inclination for such intensified and careful study of a subject as the gardener of Munstead.

She did not forget from whom she had learnt these lessons in colour, and mentions 'one who is now dead but to whom I owe, with deepest thankfulness, a precious memory of forty years of helpful and sympathetic guidance and encouragement in the observation and study of colour beauty'. This friend to whom she refers is, of course, the late H. B. Brabazon.

Probably her biggest contribution to the study of colour is that she has established that no colour stands alone and that it can only have real value if it is thought of in relation to the colours close beside it.

Here is a chunk of wisdom from page 57 of her book which rounds off the whole matter: 'But good gardening means patience and dogged determination. There must be many failures and losses, but by always pushing on there will also be the reward of success. Those who do not know are apt to think that hardy flower gardening of the best kind is easy. It is not easy at all. It has taken me half a lifetime merely to find out what is best worth doing, and a good slice of another half to puzzle out the ways of doing it.'

CHAPTER XI

1909–1919

Publication of Gardens for Small Country Houses—*The war years*—Publication of Garden Ornament

The partnership between Lutyens and Miss Jekyll never faltered, although she was occupied to a great extent with her writing at this time and kept very much now within the confines of the Munstead Wood garden, while he was busy with even bigger commissions. They still worked together and in his letters to Lady Emily there were many affectionate references to 'Bumps'.

There had been Millmead in 1906—perhaps one of their joint undertakings nearest to her heart. The restoring of Great Dixter, Sussex, in 1910 and co-operation with the work on Hampstead Garden City in the same year were both matters of consultation between them. (The planning of the crematorium gardens came a few years later, about 1915.) Lindisfarne and Lambay were rescued by the vision of Lutyens and converted into something habitable. For their difficult and precipitous gardens Miss Jekyll suggested the use of shrubs with grey foliage contrasting with a few bright colours—sea buckthorn, *Cineraria maritima*, rosemary, along with fuchsias, pinks and campions. At Lambay excavations had revealed a wide rampart wall which provided much-needed shelter, and supports of an old farm shed were used as posts for roses.

What was the secret of this lasting relationship between Lutyens and Miss Jekyll? It is a big question but, apart from his genius, the attraction to Miss Jekyll may well have been her protégé's sense of fun. Sometimes it was irritating, but more often irresistible, and Renishaw was one of the gardens where it seemed to bubble over most. Sir George Sitwell spent hours planning and re-planning the gardens of Renishaw Hall, Derbyshire. In his imagination terraces were built, dams constructed, sweeping flights of stone steps in wide curves made to connect

51. Gertrude Jekyll, from a portrait by William Nicholson, painted in 1920.

52. Octavia Hill (1838–1912), co-founder of the National Trust. Miss Jekyll was entrusted with the care of Hydon Heath, given in Octavia Hill's memory.

53. The walled forecourt before the South Front, Nymans. Miss Jekyll's advice
was reputedly given on the spring border in the walled garden.

54. Gledstone Hall, Yorkshire. 'This garden structure, supporting a distant
prospect . . . is softened by a Jekyll planting scheme. . . .'

one lake with another, with an odd island or two added as an afterthought.

The date of Miss Jekyll's intervention must have been about 1910, but Edwin Lutyens had been called in two or three years earlier. He wrote excitedly to Lady Emily: 'They want me to do the garden, ball room, billiard room, great drawing room, dining room, etc. Sir George wants to build a little water palace (one room) on the lake, which would be a delightful thing to do. . . .'[1] Sir George's ideas of laying out pools, ponds, lakes and cascades in his gardens were inclined to lead to embarrassing financial problems and most of them had to be abandoned forthwith. If they were not impossibly expensive then they were often impracticable. One of these concerned special arrangements for the cook to have her boudoir on an island in a large stretch of water. Lutyens's reaction to this may be guessed from Sir George's report: 'It was a pity,' he said, 'that architects always raised unnecessary points against their own interest, and Lutyens . . . had been in one of his silly moods the other day . . . and had blurted out that he wondered if the cook would enjoy sculling half a mile before breakfast.'[2]

The first visit to Renishaw was followed by many others, and Lutyens dealt with the mad-hatter schemes of Sir George with his usual charm and high spirits, in much the same manner as he was to deal later with the schemes of Lady Sackville.

'His sense of irreverence, his spontaneity, his hatred of the pompous, made him a perfect foil to my father', writes Sir Osbert Sitwell in *Great Morning*. His 'Jack-in-the-box forms of fun' and 'his endless, bubbling flow of puns' were directed against friends and clients alike with varying results, but few were able to resist his charm. An incident described in *Great Morning* when he was supposed to be in consultation illustrates the lightning workings of his mind. Sir George had gone to look for a drawing he had thought of for the garden, and Lutyens and Sir Osbert were left together in the room. As they were talking, the sofa they were sitting on suddenly split its covering and some of the stuffing—horsehair—came out. Without hesitation or comment Ned Lutyens pulled a bit away, got up from the sofa, tore a piece of ribbon from the edge of a curtain and tied it round the wisp. He tucked the little bundle into an envelope—all this without a word—sealed it, and wrote on it, and then placed it inside a drawer of a cabinet. He sat down again quickly, remarking: 'Nobody's likely to find that for a long time, and by then it will have become real.' Years afterwards Sir Osbert was passing this

[1] *The Life of Sir Edwin Lutyens.*
[2] *Great Morning*, by Sir Osbert Sitwell. Macmillan, 1948.

cabinet one day at Renishaw and without thinking he looked into the drawer. Inside was an envelope on which was written: 'A lock of Marie Antoinette's hair, cut from her head ten minutes after execution.'

Lutyens brought this spirit of light-hearted spontaneity into his work and especially into his dealings with Miss Jekyll. Her part in the Renishaw gardens is observed in the same book. 'This year [1911] . . . the flowers had attained a peculiar richness typical of the epoch, for Lutyens's friend and mentor, Miss Jekyll, had been sent the plan of the garden beds by my father and had issued her decrees for them: in one part they were to be filled only with blossoms of blue and orange and lemon-yellow, in another with French eighteenth-century blues and pinks.'

She is described as a 'friend and mentor' and for 'mentor' the Oxford Dictionary gives 'an experienced and trusted adviser'. This was indeed one side of the coin. On the other there was the enthusiasm of a younger man whose chief maxim about his work was: 'Architecture is building with wit.' Their relationship was a marriage of wisdom and wit. It is understandable that Miss Jekyll has been described again and again by those who can still remember her as having 'a wonderful sense of humour'. Otherwise she would not have delighted in his sense of fun or seen underneath it the genius and serious intent of his work.

Lady Emily recalls Ned Lutyens and Gertrude Jekyll dancing together in the firelight on winter evenings at Munstead Wood, and though she scolded him if she thought he was becoming too frivolous, Lady Emily says that Miss Jekyll obviously enjoyed it very much indeed.

Miss Jekyll's forbearance with his nonsense was typical of her broadness of character and speaks, too, for the charm of his method of attack when dealing with clients who might not have the same ideas as their architect. Mr Hussey writes '. . . they were almost powerless to control or amend a design once conceived. If they had come to the office prepared to make a row, within a couple of minutes his charm had mollified them, with sketched ideas for this and that and probably a dig in the ribs and "nonsense, that won't ruin you! but don't tell your wife!" '[1]

He was irresistible, but Sir Herbert Baker felt it necessary to admonish him with reference to the submission of tenders. 'Remember', he scolded, 'you cannot carry off that kind of thing with a Government as you do with private clients, with a joke!'[2]

Miss Jekyll was able to deal with this irresistible charm and 'Jack-in-the-box form of fun' in no uncertain manner, controlling it when

[1] *Life of Sir Edwin Lutyens.*   [2] Ibid.

necessary with all the firmness of her solid character, but at the same time often delighting in it. She probably also provided a feeling of security and welcome, and, in spite of the criticism, he knew she believed in his work. He loved to be with people who gave him the feeling of a home.

Miss Jekyll's botanical knowledge—though she usually denied any expert familiarity with plant names—was being stimulated over these years by visits from various gardening friends, many of them authors. Mr E. A. Bowles, now of crocus fame, may have been working on his first two books, *My Garden in Spring* and *My Garden in Summer* (published in 1914) when he visited Munstead Wood. He had already served on the Council of the Royal Horticultural Society. Miss Ellen Willmott was another visitor and friend, and one who also brought her camera, as she contributed some of the illustrations for *Children and Gardens*. Her *Genus Rosa* was just about to be published—it came out in parts during the years 1910–14, illustrated with colour plates from drawings by Alfred Parsons, A.R.A., published by John Murray. Miss Willmott dedicated this work to Queen Alexandra. Two more visitors about this time were the Countess Von Arnim, author of *Elizabeth and Her German Garden*, and Mr H. Avray Tipping, the scholarly author of *The Garden of Today* and that gigantic work, *English Homes*.

An important friendship was growing during these years with the Keeper of the Department of Botany at the British Museum, Mr James Britten. In an earlier rather brief letter she enlists Mr Britten's help: 'Will you kindly name this plant for me?' In 1910 she writes a longer and more friendly letter, this time making arrangements for Mr Britten to come to Munstead Wood in order to meet another mutual acquaintance. 'As soon as I hear from you I will write to Dr Hyland. I will do my best about the weather although some of my efforts in that direction have, of late, not met with success. . . . Remember, you are coming to a cottage with the very simplest ways—no evening clothes are allowed; only your barest necessaries in a small bag. Will you look out for my roan cob at Godalming at 5.28. . . .'

He was a bachelor, always ready for battle, argued about everything, a staunch Roman Catholic. He had a moustache and a beard, rather a squat-looking face with an alert expression in his eyes and wore glasses. He looked over these almost as much as through them and, though Keeper of Botany, declared that he could never see anything through a microscope.

Gardening was the original interest which brought them together, but in later years this friendship was to develop into a warm—in all senses of the word—relationship with the two of them and with Mr Logan Pearsall Smith on the use of words. The arguments were often hot and fierce. Mr Pearsall Smith wrote later: 'Britten was an irascible, fault-finding little man, and Miss Jekyll had no exaggerated disinclination for a scrimmage now and then. Their friendship, as with most of Britten's friendships, was a kind of cat-and-dog relationship, Britten being in this case the cat, and Miss Jekyll the big, good-natured dog, who was, however, not incapable of growling when a growl was called for.'[1]

This was the life led by Miss Jekyll in the years immediately before the Great War. In 1911 she was sixty-eight years of age, living of necessity an even more solitary life at Munstead Wood. Some of her closest friends had died and she could not, in any case, deal with many visitors; she relied on a few that she knew well or in whom she was especially interested. In the gardening world William Robinson, now seventy-two years old, was almost entirely dependent on bathchair locomotion. Reginald Farrer was probably drawing up the outline for his book, *The English Rock Garden*, full of ideas which suited well the naturalistic gardening of Mr Robinson and Miss Jekyll as opposed to the formal bedding-out gospel preached in Victorian times. In China, E. H. Wilson was working for the American Professor C. S. Sargent, curator of the world-famous Arnold Arboretum. Most of Wilson's early pioneering work had been done for the firm of Veitch of Devon and it was during September, 1911, that Miss Jekyll visited their nursery at Exeter on her return journey from a holiday in Cornwall.

1912 saw the publication of her book written in collaboration with Sir Lawrence Weaver, published by Country Life—*Gardens for Small Country Houses*. It is interesting that in the days of plenty before the outbreak of war there was this demand for ideas in planning for small properties. Even then the burden of the large estate was beginning to be felt, and greater interest in gardening shown by the owners of more moderate sized gardens.

The authors claim 'that no feature has been illustrated which would not be fitting in a small garden when reduced to scale, or which it would be wrong so to reduce'.

The opening sentence of the introductory chapter proclaims the gist of the Jekyll–Lutyens relationship: 'It is upon the right relation of the garden to the house that its value and the enjoyment that is to be derived from it will largely depend. The connection must be intimate, and the access not only convenient, but inviting.'

Another point of major importance is made in this chapter, that of

[1] *Reperusals and Recollections.* Constable.

the relation between the house and garden and the surroundings in which they are located. 'In the arrangement of any site the natural conditions of the place should first be studied. If they are emphatic or in any way distinct, they should be carefully maintained and fostered. It is grievous to see, in a place that has some well-defined natural character, that character destroyed or stultified, for it is just that quality that is most precious. Many a hillside site, such as those on wild moorland, has been vulgarised by a conventionally commonplace treatment. Such a place has possibilities that are delightful, and all the easier to accommodate because the poor soil imposes certain conditions and restricts the choice of plants. There are natural gardens in these places, and especially natural groves, that cannot be bettered in the way of consistent and harmonious planting by any choice from a nurseryman's catalogue. Such a region is a hillside clothed with juniper, holly, birch, mountain ash, scrub oak and Scotch fir, in a delightfully spontaneous grouping with undergrowths of bracken and whortleberry, and heaths in the more open spaces, and other delights of honeysuckle, wild thyme, wood sage and dwarf scabious' (p. xix). Chapter I in this book on Millmead and Chapter V on Munstead Wood have already been mentioned.

Country houses are specified in the title of the book, but some small town gardens were included, that of 100, Cheyne Walk belonging to Sir Hugh Lane being one of them. It is planned round a leaning mulberry tree and 'has a refined classical flavour without being stiff'. Professor Tonks, Wilston Steer and George Moore were frequent visitors to this house and the peace and dignity of the garden must have provided a suitable background for their many discussions. (There is a mention of Professor Tonks painting a relative of Miss Jekyll working in his garden, by Violet Hammersley: '1907–1908— Tonks spent the summer painting my husband working in his rock garden in the evenings—a garden he had made himself with loving care, being, like his cousin Gertrude Jekyll, of the tribe of born gardeners.'[1] If only he had painted the Munstead garden what a treasure we should have.)

Lutyens was also approached by Sir Hugh Lane in 1912 to produce designs for a gallery to house his famous collection of paintings. First suggested sites were in St Stephen's Green and then in Merrion Square, Dublin, but as neither of these proved to be suitable and there seemed to be no land available, they conceived the idea of spanning the Liffey with a bridge having galleries for the pictures at either end.

[1] *The London Magazine*, Vol. 3, No. 1, January, 1958.

There seems to be a faint Sitwellian ring about the plan, estimated to cost about £45,000, and Dublin during 1913 was not the place nor was it the time to ask for such a sum in order to house decently thirty-nine paintings. The corporation refused to co-operate and Sir Hugh Lane moved his pictures to the National Gallery in London. Lutyens must have been disappointed, but there were greater things already looming up on his horizon.

Following the transfer of the capital of India from Calcutta to Delhi in 1911, the most ambitious architectural programme of the British Empire was contemplated and an architect with vision and experience was needed. Lutyens had by now a good many well-received buildings behind him, among them the whole lay-out and design of the Hampstead Garden Suburb. Mr Christopher Hussey writes: 'At home he was now famous as a domestic architect of supreme skill. . . . The English conception of a good-looking house set in a gracious garden among fine trees, which he had so variously realised with the help of Miss Jekyll, raised the standard of domestic design throughout the world.'[1]

Lutyens was now forty-two and seemed to have acquired a definite trend and ideal in his work. In January, 1912, he was invited to serve on a committee of three to advise the Government of India on the designing and lay-out of the new capital. In the autumn of the same year he travelled to Delhi and during the next two years he visited many north-western frontier towns.

While Lutyens was travelling to the East Miss Jekyll's work was travelling to the West. This was a time of appreciation of her writings in America and of her growing correspondence with Mrs Francis King, a well-known American gardener writer.[2] Mrs King was one of the Founders and also a Vice-President of the Garden Club of America as well as an author of gardening literature. From Miss Jekyll's letters it is obvious that there was already a school of thought in America based on Munstead ideas. Mrs King paid Miss Jekyll the compliment of asking her to write a Preface to her book being published in 1913, *The Garden Day By Day*. (Much later, in 1932, Mrs King contributed a chapter on American Gardens to that excellent work, *The Story Of The Garden* by Eleanour Sinclair Rohde.)

Miss Jekyll, meanwhile, was occupied at Munstead Wood, sending plans for other people's gardens and working in her own. There were

[1] *The Life of Sir Edwin Lutyens.*
[2] She was awarded the George Robert White Medal of Honor by the Massachusetts Horticultural Society.

more days when visitors to the Munstead garden had to be turned away and there were more signs of fatigue by the end of the day. In the evenings the making of shell pictures took the place of finer work which might strain her eyes.

None of this meant, however, a lessening of her interest in the plans of gardens on which she could give advice, even if it was not possible to visit them in person. There was the case of Miss Baring, another cousin of Miss Jekyll, whose garden was in the New Forest. A friend who went to look after it found it well laid out and thoughtfully planned, with two fine Scotch pines left standing in a good position and planted underneath with ericas and azaleas. 'Gertrude wouldn't come here', explained Miss Baring, 'as she was getting old, but she made me send her a measured ground plan, which I had to get a surveyor to do, as I couldn't make one myself. Then she arranged it all.' Miss Baring was not herself knowledgeable about flowers, but she wanted a good garden and so she sent a list of fairly elementary questions to Miss Jekyll. These came back with some downright replies such as 'nonsense' or 'don't be silly' or 'do use your head and consult my chart'.[1]

There may have been physical fatigue and acute myopia but her mind was as lively and as alert as ever.

Two other garden designs were put in hand just before the outbreak of war, both closely connected with her home. One was for a memorial cloister erected to the memory of the heroic wireless operator Jack Phillips who went down on the *Titanic* in 1912, and who came from Godalming. The other was a design and lay-out of a tract of land about two miles from Munstead Wood which had been acquired by the National Trust in memory of its founder, Octavia Hill. She also had died in 1912 (Plate 52).

The first of these two schemes was undertaken by Mr Thackeray Turner, a well-known gardener, and Miss Jekyll's advice was required in the selection of evergreen shrubs and plants suitable to the restraint of its architectural setting. The second gave her greater scope of a kind which especially appealed to her. A piece of natural, open ground required controlling without formalising. Tracks through the plantation were needed in place of the old rabbit-runs, and she is recorded as working with a patrol of Boy Scouts in 1915 to clear away the undergrowth and arrange a system of neat paths leading to the highest point, about five hundred feet—from which there was a commanding view of the beautiful unspoilt country of West Surrey. This clearing away of low-growing tangled bushes was a big thing to tackle over such

[1] *Bricks and Flowers*, by Katherine Everett. Constable, 1949.

an area at her time of life—she was now just over seventy years of age —and the work went on twice a week during the spring and summer with energy which even surprised herself.

The lights had gone out over Europe; the *Lusitania*, torpedoed in the Atlantic; the Dardanelles expedition; the war in Mesopotamia; these were some of the headlines splashed across the newspapers of 1915. Miss Jekyll, alert in spite of her years and her failing sight, worked with parties to collect spagnum moss which was needed at the Front, helped to supply the military hospital at Thorncombe with fruit and vegetables grown in beds usually given up to flowers, and conducted Canadian soldiers from a near-by camp round her Munstead garden.

An activity dating back from her student days came to the fore again in the spring of 1916. Miss Jekyll had often visited the Victoria and Albert Museum as a young woman to study and to paint. Then, on her travels abroad and especially to Algiers, she had begun to make a collection of materials and sometimes garments relating to local costume. On 23rd May, Lady Horner wrote to Mr Kendrick, Keeper of Textiles at the Victoria and Albert Museum, mentioning a 'very beautiful old quilt' which Miss Jekyll was ready to give to the Museum if it would be suitable, and suggesting that he should go down to Munstead to see her 'as she has lots of things put away!'

A week later Mr Kendrick visited Munstead Wood and went through her collection with her. A considerable number of articles were selected to be given to the Museum, including the quilt (seventeenth-century Portuguese), several pieces of Algerian embroidery, Oriental and European details of costume and some Italian embroideries. She writes in a letter on 14th June, 1916:

Dear Mr Kendrick,

I am glad to include the two copies of monks' frocks in the case which I have finished packing today and which will be put on the rail for the goods train tonight. The larger, brown one I made myself in around the year 1895 from one I borrowed from one of the convents in Sussex—I do not remember which—of a Franciscan or allied order. I borrowed it for use with a model. The other, white one was given me by my old friend Mdme Bodichon—a Sussex woman and artist, and is likely to be correct.

I came upon a few other articles after your visit and ventured to include them for your consideration—but if I have sent anything that is useless it might be returned.

It is a great satisfaction to me to know that so many of the items I had to offer are acceptable to the Museum.

Yours very truly,
Gertrude Jekyll.

This was only another sideline of all her many interests, but it was probably due to her artistic training that she was able to make a selection of these items worthy of inclusion in a collection for the Victoria and Albert Museum, in just the same way that she knew instinctively which plants to select for her garden and where to put them.

'Few men with a remarkable sense of life run along tram lines. They are always turning off their road even if their objective stays considerably in view. Always something is intriguing them. Always that something can be put to the general account, can be added to the general unity by which they are possessed. . . . Parkinson and Miller were not tram-liners . . . they were men of appetite and curiosity. I do not believe that a great gardener was ever gardener alone, any more than the great or good poets and painters were concerned only with poems or pictures. . . .'[1]

An example was Monsieur Le Nôtre: '. . . but his training for Versailles was not in grafting rose-trees or layering gillyflowers. He studied first to be a painter, an enthusiasm which never left him, for he collected many fine pictures, especially by Poussin, who, as we might guess, was his favourite artist.'[2] Again, Joseph Paxton advised young gardeners to study other subjects than gardening, especially poetry, the arts and literary composition. The mention of poetry reminds one hat it was a poet laureate who was one of the first people to use the term 'landscape gardening'.

'I have used the term "landscape gardener" because, in accordance with our present-day taste, every good landscape painter is the proper designer of gardens.'[3]

In Miss Jekyll's books there are quotations which show a wide variety in her reading—from George Herbert, William Cobbett, John Evelyn, William Robinson and, of course, Ruskin. Her appreciation of Ruskin had no obvious connection with gardening. It was based on his ideas about painting, about social conditions, and about Greek studies.

[1] *Gardenage,* by Geoffrey Grigson. Routledge and Kegan Paul, 1952.
[2] *Men and Gardens,* by Nan Fairbrother. Hogarth Press, 1956.
[3] *Unconnected Thoughts on Gardening,* by William Shenstone (1764).

'But elegance, chief grace the garden shows
And most attractive, is the fair result
Of thought, the creature of a polish'd mind.' (William Cowper)

and, again:

'Virgil does not speak of the beauty of ducks swimming in a river, the softness of their voices and their round black eyes so intelligent, but I should not have known how beautiful they are when swimming in a river if I had not read Virgil . . .'

Heloise and Abelard.
(George Moore translation)

Miss Jekyll was no 'tram-liner'.

A summer holiday with the Lutyens family at Folly Farm in the Kennet valley in 1916 is mentioned by Mr Hussey. 'Even Bumps was coaxed away from Munstead Wood and, after doing a little gardening by force of habit, would take off her hob-nailed boots to play the pianola'.[1]

Edwin Lutyens himself had returned from Delhi in March of this year, renewing especially at this time his friendship with Lady Sackville. Her appetite for fun matched his, as well as her interest in extravagant conversions of houses—like the three adjacent houses in Sussex Square, Brighton, converted into one large dwelling with, among other commodities, a dining room capable of seating one hundred guests, 'though she never had more than two and took all her meals in a loggia'.[2]

Lady Sackville was middle-aged and rather fat, but her face is described as having 'an almost classical prettiness, and her expression could be extremely seductive'.[3] She loved to watch his drawings as 'with jokes pouring endlessly from his lips, he flung domes and towers into the air, decorated them with her monogram, raised fountains and pavilions. . . .'[4] She lavished gifts upon him. One of them was a Rolls-Royce which had been a longed-for dream for many years. It was a pity that it was the more superficial side of his nature and his work which she encouraged. He needed sympathy and interest, but he needed much more the stern guidance of a 'Bumps'. Unfortunately 'Bumps' was not at an age to be on the spot in London and it must be admitted, in any case, that when Lutyens took Lady Sackville to visit Miss Jekyll at Munstead Wood in the autumn of 1916, she was

---

[1] *Life of Sir Edwin Lutyens.*   [2] Ibid.
[3] *Great Morning*, by Sir Osbert Sitwell.   [4] *Life of Sir Edwin Lutyens.*

'immediately charmed by her'. However, sterner things lay ahead.

In 1917 Lutyens was invited to travel, with Sir Herbert Baker and Charles Aitkin, to the battlefields of France and there to decide on the form of military cemeteries and monuments to be adopted. He wrote feelingly to Lady Emily: 'What humanity can endure, suffer, is beyond belief.' Montreuil, Abbeville . . . miles of country where he saw 'ribbons of little crosses each touching each across a cemetery—set in a wilderness of annuals—and where one sort of flower has grown the effect is charming, easy, and oh so pathetic, that one thinks no other monument is needed'.[1]

Lutyens sent in a suggestion for every British cemetery to have one great stone of good proportions raised up on steps, facing towards the east with the graves lying before it, and having some 'fine thought or words of sacred dedication' inscribed indelibly on it. It is significant that in this he turned to Bumps for criticism or suggestions or confirmation. Mr Hussey records that 'by mid-August Miss Jekyll had written to him at length, endorsing his Great Stone conception. . .'.[2]

Towards the end of the war Miss Jekyll submitted planting schemes for the British cemeteries in France. She was directly responsible to the chairman of the Imperial War Graves Commission in her choice of flowers and plants, some of which she had cared for in her own garden. White thrift was one of the plants selected, numbers of which were packed and sent off to the Commission's offices.

On 1st January, 1918, Edwin Lutyens received his knighthood. The day before it was announced the new knight was travelling by train, alone in his carriage, through the Pyrenees in intense cold on his way to design a house for the Duke of Penaranda. He wrote to Lady Emily in his usual 'fooling' style: 'We are snowed up at Avila, three hours from Madrid, snow banks in front, a derailed train behind, our fuel for warming the carriage failed, the lights went out, and there for hours on a mountain top I waited . . . thoroughly be-knighted!! It snows and snows, I with a fearful cold in mysnose—it was all s'nose, as my mouchoir s'knows too well!'[3]

Miss Jekyll must have felt gratified at this recognition for her protégé. She had greatly influenced his ideas and some of the biggest commissions had come his way either through her recommendation or on account of domestic architecture carried out in partnership with her. Smug or complacent she would never be, but on her own account, too, she had reason to feel satisfaction. She had come to the position in her life of knowing that what she set out to do would be accomplished.

[1] *Life of Sir Edwin Lutyens.*   [2] Ibid.   [3] Ibid.

Much of her success was due to her artistic training and to her innate good taste but, as Mr Falkner observed, it also required 'the energy of the ant, the perseverance of the spider, the unwavering pursuit of an idea, undeterred by a thousand failures and uninfluenced by any outward tendency she did not choose to notice'. In 1918 *Garden Ornament* was published—a folio book fully illustrated, and a worthy companion to *Gardens for Small Country Houses*. It was a forerunner of the sumptious garden books which appear today, confirming the fact that photographs educate and make suggestions.

Towards the end of the year came the Armistice, but the privations of a country at war were not over. Ration books did not disappear overnight and the cost of living was high. Writing to Mrs King in April, 1919, Miss Jekyll came the nearest to a grouse or complaint that she ever uttered. She described her altered way of life, illness, almost blindness and general lack of strength. But she characteristically expressed thanks that it was only for herself she felt this inconvenience and not for a family. 'What happens to an old woman does not really matter and if it must be, I shall face it quite cheerfully as my way of paying for the war and its good ending. I am afraid this is rather a growl. . . .'

And then came the Cenotaph. Mr Robert Lutyens writes: 'On July 19th, 1919, Lloyd George summoned my father and told him that the Government wished to erect a "catafalque" for the anniversary of the Armistice. He explained that it must be undenominational in character, as commemorating men of every creed, and, in the first instance, was envisaged as a temporary structure; hence, no doubt, Lloyd George's choice of the word "catafalque" as indicating a "temporary stage or platform erected by way of honour in a church to receive a coffin or effigy. . . .".'[1]

Now we must go back many years to an occasion at Munstead Wood when Miss Jekyll asked Ned Lutyens to build her a seat for the garden incorporating a large bulk of wood with supports of masonry. On its completion Charles Liddell, their friend, remarked on its similarity to the Cenotaph of Sigismunda. Lutyens did not know the word, 'and elicited that it meant an empty tomb, "a monument erected to a deceased person whose body is buried elsewhere"'. Shortly afterwards he jokingly explained to Herbert Jekyll that the new object in the garden was 'a cenotaph to Bumps'.[2] Miss Jekyll refers to it in *Home and Garden*, mentioning that it is much appreciated by her cat Pinkieboy and his friends who liked to enjoy the full afternoon sun for the mid-day

[1] *Sir Edwin Lutyens: An Appreciation in Perspective.*   [2] Ibid.

snooze or, later in the day, the alternate light of sunshine and shadow filtering through the tall silver birch branches (Plate 46).

Robert Lutyens went on: 'Father immediately remembered the long-ago incident of the "cenotaph to Bumps" and evolved the design, not as a catafalque but, infinitely more apt, as the empty tomb—the monument of millions "buried elsewhere". No one would connect this apparently most abstract and formal conception with a picturesque Surrey garden. Nor would anybody but my father have remembered the incident so vividly for thirty years, assimilated its significance, and been able, when the time came, to give it seemingly spontaneous architectural form.'[1]

It is understandable that Lutyens' reply to Lloyd George was 'not a catafalque but a Cenotaph'. There was need for quick thinking as it was required in position in Whitehall by the end of the month for the Peace celebrations. All the same, the extraordinary speed with which the plan was conceived and delivered could hardly have been anticipated by Lloyd George when he asked for it. The design was worked out that same day, a rough drawing done that evening on the back of an advertisement to show to the Hon. Mrs Harold Nicolson with whom Lutyens was dining, and the half-inch and full-size working drawings were at 10 o'clock the next morning in the hands of the Office of Works.

Mr Christopher Hussey writes: 'It can be said that the commissioning, conception, and rough though finite design of the Cenotaph took place within six hours; probably less.'

The story of the origin of the memorial and the train of thought which led him to suggest the name of Cenotaph was related to Mr Hussey by Lutyens himself. In order to be quite sure of all the details, Mr Hussey asked him to go over the details again. Lutyens confirmed them all, showing that his design and interpretation stemmed from the Sigismunda at Munstead Wood.

Mr Robert Lutyens enumerates further the different factors which helped to make up this composite picture of the Cenotaph: 'His [father's] receptiveness to a fresh idea, though it may have seemed a trifling archaeological detail at the time; his immense memory for anything bearing on architecture; the peculiar cast of his mind, which would attach a clear image to any word once understood; the nature and extent of his debt to Miss Jekyll and her fastidiously civilised circle, which goes far deeper than any mere picturesque orientation. . . .'[2]

The work on the permanent monument was started in October, 1919,

[1] *Sir Edwin Lutyens: An Appreciation in Perspective.*   [2] Ibid.

and finished in time for the second Anniversary of Peace the next year. There was one letter of appreciation, among many, which must have given him special pleasure:

My dear Lutyens,

The Cenotaph grows in beauty as one strolls down alone o' nights to look at it, which becomes my habit. I stand cogitating how and why it is so noble a thing. It is how the war has moved you and lifted you above yourself. I think it was Milton who described poetry as 'thoughts that voluntarily move harmonious numbers'. This is a harmonious number and I feel proud of it and you.

Yours sincerely,
J. M. Barrie.[1]

Miss Jekyll wrote: 'The name [Cenotaph of Sigismunda] was so undoubtedly suitable to the monumental mass of elm and to its somewhat funereal environment of weeping birch and spire-like mullein, that it took hold at once, and the Cenotaph of Sigismunda it will always be as long as I am alive to sit on it.'[2] She could have had little idea then what significance this would have in later years or of how the mood of sadness and dignity of the weeping trees from a corner of her Surrey garden would help to inspire a great memorial for the nation. In a letter of appreciation to Lutyens Lloyd George wrote: 'The Cenotaph by its very simplicity fittingly expresses the memory in which the people hold all those who so bravely fought and died for the country.'[3]

[1] *The Life of Edwin Lutyens.*   [2] *Home and Garden*, p. 71.
[3] *The Life of Sir Edwin Lutyens.*

CHAPTER XII

1920–1921

A portrait

William Nicholson had been a personal friend of Ned Lutyens since the turn of the century and for the last three years he had been a neighbour in Apple Tree Yard, the mews cottage of 7, St James's Square, where Lutyens had the Delhi office. He was an established painter and 'with the end of the war . . . his creative energy found fresh force. Generally speaking the still life pictures continued to follow the old pattern of glowing colours set against a dark background, as did the portraits, which included the well-known one of Miss Gertrude Jekyll.'[1]

It was through Lutyens that she was eventually persuaded to sit for William Nicholson, which was an achievement in itself. She was at first not only reluctant, but horrified at the idea, saying that she was not a paintable kind of person and that she could not spare the time. The persuasive charm of her old friend and the adaptability of the artist won the day and throughout most of October and November of 1920 the rather unofficial 'sittings' took place. In most of them the painter was condemned to work in lamplight, as she would not spare the best hours of light when she could herself be working. In the intervals, Nicholson turned his attention to an old pair of gardening boots, using for them the valuable daylight which she refused to waste on herself.

The portrait was exhibited at the Grafton Gallery in the next spring and may now be seen in the National Portrait Gallery, neighbour to that of Henry James, who was born in the same year as Miss Jekyll. Her portrait was exhibited by the National Portrait Society, first in London and then at Nottingham in 1933, Belfast in 1934, and at the National Gallery, 1942. It was formerly in the possession of Sir Edwin Lutyens, who handed it over to the Tate in 1922. It is now on permanent loan to the National Portrait Gallery. In this portrait she 'is sitting

[1] *William Nicholson,* by Lilian Browse. Rupert Hart-Davis, 1956.

143

in an arm-chair, facing left, hands in front of her, with fingers touching'.

It seems an interesting coincidence that Miss Jekyll and Henry James should hang next to each other, both born the same year, both un-married, both authors of books showing exceptional knowledge and understanding of children. The books are written from quite different angles—Miss Jekyll's addressed to children, whereas Henry James's *What Maisie Knew* shows the workings of a child's mind in the complex adult situation of divorce—but they both reveal extraordinary in-sight into what a child might feel about sadness, delight and adventure, respectively.

The portrait is important as a work of art, but also on account of its picture of Miss Jekyll's character. The artist wrote that he hoped he had put 'a little of her serene charm' into the painting. But the portrait of the boots has, in some ways, become almost more significant. Miss Jekyll's boots have acquired over the years the position of a kind of symbol in the gardening world. A conversation between a young man and woman in *The Barber's Clock*,[1] illustrates this:

' "Do you know her [Miss Jekyll's] portrait at the Tate Gallery?"

' "Yes", said Jenny, "so wise and comfortable."

' "And the portrait of her boots by the same painter," said Richard. "Have you seen that? The boots of one who loves the soil and under-stands it. . . ." '

In an argument on formal and natural gardening—which to prefer, the Robinsonian wilderness and the natural garden or the deliberate artifice of Schloss Bruhl, near Cologne—Geoffrey Grigson writes of nature as the gardener's opponent: 'She sneaks in, she inserts her weeds, her couch-grass, her ground elder, her plaintain, her greenfly. . . . If I did not remember that I was human and also a part of nature, I should have poisoned her one day along with the weeds . . . and I should have put in her grave my guide to Stourhead, Wordsworth's poems, and Gertrude Jekyll's boots.'[2]

But to return to the portrait of Miss Jekyll and all that it shows—William Nicholson spoke of 'her serene charm' and he also expressed gratitude for the opportunity to paint 'so lovable a character'. She has been presented sometimes as being 'formidable' and autocratic. Mr Falkner wrote: 'I believe some people found G.J. autocratic. To me she seemed the most modest and the meekest of gardeners. She was never tired of telling of her failures with onions and would even admit that anemones and phlox were nearly heartbreaking.' In another letter he describes her as 'the complete vanquisher of all her adversaries', but

[1] *The Barber's Clock*, by E. V. Lucas. Methuen, 1931. [2] *Gardenage*.

55. Great Dixter. Plantings of grey-foliaged plants, with interesting juxtaposition of different-shaped foliage plants.

GARDENS OPEN TO THE PUBLIC, THAT SHOW THE JEKYLL INFLUENCE

56. Wisley, with many plantings mentioned by Miss Jekyll in her books, especially the fine clumps of gunnera.

57. Deanery Garden, Sonning, showing Jekyll plantings of the Banksian rose, *Solanum jasminoides* up an east wall, lavender hedges, roses growing up into fruit trees, etc.

58. The grey and white garden at Sissinghurst. This garden shows the Jekyll influence in many of its aspects—primroses under hazels, cottage-style design, roses trained up into fruit trees, etc.

59. Wisley. Part of the rock garden. Miss Jekyll helped to lay the stones for this part of the garden, and made some comment on the arrangement of the plants. 'Mr Wilson stopped, and looking at me straight with a kindly smile, said very quietly "That is your business, not mine".'

goes on: 'That anyone with her magnificent urbanity could have had an adversary may seem absurd, but it was so. She could differ decidedly, promptly and completely, and she was sometimes not in the least disinclined to show it.'

Mr Herbert Cowley writes: '. . . I had my knuckles rapped on occasion, but for all that I worshipped her. Miss Jekyll was not difficult —oh, no, but she sometimes had difficult folk to deal with, especially publishers who wanted to improve upon her script and titles. She had a lively sense of humour. . . .'

Mr Cowley describes other editors who would go to great lengths not to cut or chop about her beautifully written English. There was the predicament of a *Country Life* editor faced with the problem of fitting into his lay-out an article by Miss Jekyll which exceeded his space by three and a half lines. Any ordinary contribution would have been cut. 'But', he related, 'I would rather have clipped the wings of an arch-angel', and he did, in fact, re-arrange the whole of the lay-out so that it all went in. Miss Musgrave remembers especially her sense of humour. 'She didn't suffer fools gladly, but she took great trouble with anyone who was really interested and she was nice to young children. She was plain to look at but charming to be with. She had what we call "the root of the matter".'

She is described alternately as 'gentle' and 'fierce'. She could be either. She had little patience with indifference or stupidity, and could settle both with quiet, but devastating remarks. She loved a jaunt or a 'treat' as children would say, and one of her passions was for playing the pianola. She was deeply, but unfussily, religious. She could say 'Forgive us our Christmases as we forgive them that Christmas against us', being supremely irritated by the sending of numerous cards to people 'for whom she felt no affection and hardly knew' and vice versa. She had a keen sense of fun and delight in adventure with children, understanding their love of magic and make-believe.

If all this is linked together there emerges a composite picture which has been clearly caught by William Nicholson. She sits in her chair, a stout, round figure, dressed in her usual style of voluminous blue serge: 'I remember her in her eighties, a dumpy figure in a heavy gardener's apron, her vitality shining from a face half concealed by two pairs of spectacles and a battered and yellowed straw hat'.[1] Lady Emily Lutyens says: 'There was only one kind of dress she could really wear, and it was often largely concealed by an apron and finished off by her solid gardening boots. She had beautiful hands and a delicious

[1] *The Education of a Gardener*, by Russel Page. Collins, 1962.

chuckling laugh.' Mr Oliver Hill remembers her as 'lumpy, physically, but light and witty in conversation—she was delicious'. Mrs Barnes-Brand describes her as 'having great poise together with a wonderful sense of humour. Miss Jekyll was tremendously human and most helpful if she thought you were really interested.' And in spite of all the hard work accomplished and her respect for the good use of time she still 'gave a feeling of repose'. Mr Falkner goes on: 'Someone somewhere has talked of a "little old lady". G.J. was not little bodily or in any other way. She must have been, when I first knew her, some five feet ten and weighed ten or twelve stone; with rather a deep voice but not at all masculine, without the slightest gush, capable of considerable tenderness, always putting people at their ease or keeping them there, always thinking, contriving, giving or storing information. . . .'

The no-nonsense side of her character could and did give way to the artist, and the poetry in her writing breaks through the hard core of facts and plain statements of actual experience.

'While May is still young, cowslips are in beauty on the chalk lands. . . .'
'There comes a day towards the end of March when there is but little wind, and that is from the west. . . .'
'How endlessly beautiful is woodland in winter. Today there is a thin mist; just enough to make a background of tender blue mystery. . . .'

All this William Nicholson has brought into his portrait. But, unfortunately, there cannot be seen in the picture a piece of string hanging from the back of the chair. It must be there, I think, but would hardly be a necessary component of the painting. On the other hand, it would give an important clue to one side of her character. 'I hope', said an old friend of Miss Jekyll's, 'that you have mentioned her cats'. Lady Emily wrote: 'Bumps has about six cats, three quite kittens, and they romped about the room',[1] and it was Lady Emily who told me that there was always a long piece of string hanging down from the back of Miss Jekyll's chair. At first, the point of this string was not clear until it was found to have a cork at the end of it which, of course, proved to be a perpetual attraction to whichever cats were present with the family.

Miss Jekyll loved cats. Perhaps it is a characteristic of women who live alone. Florence Nightingale 'always had four or five cats in the room, they lay on her pillow, curled themselves round her neck, upset

[1] *A Blessed Girl*, by Lady Emily Lutyens. Rupert Hart-Davis, 1953.

her ink and left paw marks on her paper'.[1] Miss Jekyll's favourite colouring for a cat was tabby with white fronts and paws. Such a tabby, with gleaming coat and spotlessly kept white patches, was Pinkieboy. She describes a typical encounter with him in the garden: 'It is a perfect summer day, and I sit looking down one of the broad turf rides in the copse and see a dark object slowly approaching. By the solemnity of the stately advance I know it must be Pinkieboy. . . . When we meet after an unusual separation of a few hours, as he sees me coming he prepares himself for a good five minutes of pleasant conversation. Its subject is always the same, namely, unqualified admiration and approval of Pinkieboy.'[2] Miss Jekyll described cats as her 'dear companions both inside and out'. She always found them 'kindly, appreciative and grateful for friendly notice' and of all the large number that she had no two 'have been the least alike'.

It is said that for Miss Jekyll, one of the attractions of visiting Mr William Robinson at his home was that close to Gravetye there was an inn called the 'Tabby Cat', thought to be the only one of that name in the country. As there were also the attractions of his garden, his collection of shrubs and his collection of paintings, which included eight Fantin-Latours, two Corots and a Van Huysum, one feels this may be stretching a point. But one might guess that cats, painting and gardening were all equally close to her heart.

In *Children and Gardens*, Gertrude Jekyll writes delightful descriptions of most of her favourite cats. There are pen pictures of Tabby—he used to love to lie in her garden basket, and one day, bringing home an especially good collection of hydrangeas, she turned away for a minute only to find, on looking back again, that Tabby had made himself a soft bed among them. Another time, 'he had made himself so comfortable' on some photographic plates which were lying in a palm leaf basket that she 'could not bear to disturb him'. Another day his selection for a lazy resting-place would be a bank of Cerastium. 'This he thinks is just suitable for his bed!' Miss Jekyll often found him there and concludes: 'though it is not quite the best thing for the Cerastium, I cannot help admiring his rich tabby coat . . .'[3] Then there was Blackie, who skipped with delight in and out of the catmint, and Tittlebat who came from the Isle of Wight. Pinkie has already been introduced, and Tavy, who had the odd habit of puffing out his tail when he was pleased. 'Tavy makes a beautiful tail when we are playing together, and he is quite pleased with himself and with me.'

---

[1] *Florence Nightingale*, by Cecil Woodham-Smith. Constable, 1950.
[2] *Home and Garden*, p. 257.   [3] *Children and Gardens*, p. 99.

One of the most endearing stories about Miss Jekyll and her cats is that of the tea-party organised for her small niece of nine years old who was staying with her during one winter. It is sometimes difficult to think of some excitement for a child in the country if the weather is bad, and Miss Jekyll had the brilliant idea of arranging a party for the cats as a special treat for the little girl before she returned home.

The idea received full approval and plans were immediately discussed, as the party had to be arranged for the next afternoon.

The menu was the first consideration. Fresh herrings were to be one of the main dishes, and so these were sent for and boiled so that they would be ready in time. Then invitations were to be issued, running something like this: 'Miss Jekyll, at home 4 o'clock. Mr Pinkieboy'. These were delivered to various guests that afternoon, and, as it was cold and wet, they were all found indoors quite easily (Plate 47).

The next afternoon there was great activity. No more trouble could have been taken if the Queen had been coming to tea. Two kittens were included in the invitations, and for them specially small saucers were provided. 'First a thick strip of fish was laid right across each saucer; an equal strip of cold rice pudding met it transversely, forming a cross-shaped figure that left four spaces in the angles. Thick cream was poured into these spaces, and the solid portion was decorated with tiny balls of butter, one rather larger in the middle, and two smaller on each of the rays.'[1] In readiness for second helpings, there was put aside a reserve supply of cream and fish.

Soon it was time for the guests to arrive, and the grown-ups present were no less excited than the little girl. Stools had been put round a small, low table, and the cats were placed in a sitting position on the stools with their paws resting on the table. This was thought to be the most comfortable position for them. No flowers were arranged in the centre of the table as it was decided, after careful consideration, to leave this free for the kittens. The whole party went off without a hitch, only slight hesitation being shown by Miss Maggie whose good manners made her feel that it might seem discourteous to put her paws on the table-cloth. However, this difficulty was soon swept away, and the food was greatly appreciated by one and all.

Pinkieboy finished first, licking his saucer completely clean and then, to make quite sure of not missing anything, his whiskers.

Great satisfaction was shown by all the guests—'there was a grand purring and washing of paws and faces'—leaving no doubt in the minds of the hostesses that all their trouble had been well worth while.

[1] *Home and Garden*, p. 267.

Obviously their choice of food for the menu, their selection of guests and their arrangements for the catering had all been quite perfect.

This story illustrates, of course, something much deeper even than Miss Jekyll's love of cats. It illustrates her love of children, and shows the reasons for her success with them. Perhaps she applied the same kind of technique to animals and children. She treated them both as individuals, with minds and opinions of their own. She had respect for their ideas and never talked down to them. She even brackets them together in her writings: 'I am sure', she says, 'that cats have a strong sense of fun, and, like children, love the delights of make-believe.'

CHAPTER XIII

Favourite Flowers

A list compiled from her first book Wood and Garden

'What favourite flowers are mine, I cannot say—
My fancy changes with the summer's day.
Sometimes I think, agreeing with the bees,
That my best flowers are those tall apple trees. . . .
Sometimes I think the columbine has won
Who hangs her head and never looks the sun
Straight in the face . . .
Sometimes I think the rose must have her place—
And then the lily shakes her golden dice
Deep in a silver cup. . . .'

Flowers, W. H. Davies

'In later days her planting of spring flowers and shrubs was especially happy. Some day I trust there will be a list given of those she loved most.' Mr Edward Woodall expresses this hope in his notes of memories of Miss Jekyll.

It is difficult to make a list; there were so many favourites. Perhaps, as the suggestion was made by Mr Woodall, a plant which he selected particularly should be mentioned first. 'She and I had a special love for those fine plants called Yuccas, as combining both bold evergreen leaves and noble spikes of flower.'

Miss Jekyll herself says: 'They are good to look at at all times of the year because of their grand strong foliage, and are the glory of the garden when in flower.'[1]

Any list of favourite flowers and shrubs would have to consider the value of smell, as Miss Jekyll refers constantly to the difference that scent makes. In describing the kalmia, which was certainly one of her favourite shrubs, she adds sadly that, though the flower is so beautiful in shape and colour, it has very little smell. 'The sweet scents of a

[1] *Wood and Garden*, p. 91.

150

garden are by no means the least of its many delights,'[1] she writes; and mentioning those to be hoped for in early spring she continues: 'the first scent of the year's first primrose is no small pleasure'.

'Smelling stirs the mind more deeply than seeing or hearing.' It seems likely that Miss Jekyll would have agreed with W. H. Hudson as to the 'seeing' towards the end of her life when her eyesight was becoming more and more inadequate. But, as to the hearing, she goes on: 'As if by way of compensation I have very keen hearing . . . many birds I am aware of only by the sound of their flight. I can nearly always tell what trees I am near by the sound of the wind in their leaves.'

There were certain sounds which Miss Jekyll liked to have in her garden and others she would not include. Particularly she loved the 'murmur of Scotch firs both near and far . . . the giant grasses, reeds and bamboo sound curiously dry [she was especially fond of bamboo and liked to plant *Lilium auratum* among it]. The great reed makes more noise in a moderate breeze than when the wind blows a gale. . . . the Arabs say, "It whispers in the breeze and is silent in the storm" '.[2]

And so Miss Jekyll's list of flowers will not only depend on the colour and shape of the flower. She walked and worked in her garden observant of details, with a feeling for scent and smell and with an appreciation of sound. It was not just the flowering season of a plant which interested her. She noticed the beauty of the stem or the leaves or the structure quite as much as the beauty of the flower.

It would be not only difficult, but impossible to give a list of all the roses, lilies, primulas and paeonies which Miss Jekyll would have chosen as favourites. She has written complete books on roses and lilies respectively; her primrose garden under the oaks and hazels is famous, and her list of selected paeonies alone in *Wood and Garden* number twenty-four. In any case, Mr Woodall specifies 'spring flowers and shrubs', which makes this difficult task a little less considerable. However, when I have come across a special mention of a particular favourite which is not either a spring flower or a shrub, as for example, in the case of Love-in-a-Mist, I have included it.

Also, as it would be impracticable to go through all her work in this connection owing to the number of flowers that would have to be recorded, I have decided on *Wood and Garden*, her first book, from which to make a selection. She may not have thought when she wrote it that she would ever write another. (In the Introduction to her next one,

---

[1] *Wood and Garden*, p. 229.   [2] *Home and Garden*, p. 279.

Home and Garden, she mentions the fact that it is because of the encouragement received from the reception of this first book that it was considered advisable to follow it up.) This being the case, it seems reasonable to conclude that most of her favourite flowers and shrubs would have been included. There is one other reason for including the flowers from this book. In a letter to Lady Emily, Edwin Lutyens remarked that 'Bumps . . . says . . . that all the best she has written about flower borders is in the chapter called Flower Garden and Pergola in *Wood and Garden*'.

As Miss Jekyll has shown in all her work an especial taste for cottage garden flowers, it will not be surprising to find many names among her list which some gardeners, conversant probably with more exotic and perhaps later and bigger editions of flowers that she knew, might find ordinary. Mignonette, which should have 'small but scented spires', is an example of this.[1] In an article written in 1929, entitled *Garden Plants of Seventy Years Ago*, Miss Jekyll regretfully mentions mignonette. 'For mignonette is and always should be a plant of modest colouring and sweetest scent; both these charming qualities belong to the older kind and have been lost, or at any rate regrettably reduced in the modern named varieties.'

Admittedly there is sometimes a good reason for what is described as 'an improved variety'. It may be more hardy and less critical of its soil conditions. But often these are not the considerations—they are the ones of bigger and brighter flowers with or without scent.

In defending the flower as it used to be, Miss Jekyll is trying to preserve some of the old favourites for the garden. Her gospel is that 'bigger' is not necessarily 'better'.

She sums up her whole attitude to the matter: 'I do most strongly urge that beauty of the highest class should be the aim, and not anything of the nature of fashion or "fancy", and that every effort should be made towards the raising rather than the lowering of the standard of taste.'[2]

There will be wild flowers as well as cottage garden flowers in Miss Jekyll's list. She writes of 'the wood-sorrel, tenderest and loveliest of wood plants' and '. . . the pretty wood-sage that will flower in the full summer . . . the little cinquefoil with a flower like a small wild strawberry . . . and dog-violets and stitchwort, and here and there is a fine clump of burdock, whose grandly formed leaves with their boldly

[1] *The Garden*, by V. Sackville-West. Michael Joseph, 1946.
[2] *Home and Garden*, p. 58.

waved edges I always think worthy of a place in a garden'.[1] There is a whole chapter devoted to honeysuckle. 'No other flowering thing that I know leaps and laughs as . . . the woodbine.'[2]

In *Colour Schemes for the Flower Garden* she refers to rescuing a seedling of the wild clematis taking root among some briars. 'I pulled it forward towards the steps, training one or two shoots to run along the hollow of the step and laying on them pieces of stone . . . to keep them from being dislodged by the skirts of visitors or the gambols of my cats.' Again, with wild thyme creeping out of the grass on to the stone: 'Luckily I just saved it from the tidying process that threatened it, and as it is now well established over the stone I still have the pleasure of its bright rosy bloom when the duties of the mowing machine rob me of the other tiny flowers—hawkweed, milkwort and bedstraw— that bloom so bravely in the intervals between its ruthless but indispensable ministrations.'[3]

List of flowers and shrubs mentioned particularly in *Wood and Garden*, to which book the page numbers refer (except Kalmia).

Amelanchier. '. . . is more beautiful when growing at its own will in high woods' (p. 52).
Andromeda floribunda (Pieris floribunda). '. . . . in beauty' (p. 50).
Anemone fulgens. '. . . is a grand cutting flower' (p. 57).
Auriculas. 'I know nothing better for pure beauty of varied colouring among early flowers' (p. 54).
Auricula. 'The actual sweetness . . . has a kind of veiled mystery' (p. 230).
Berberis (Mahonia) aquifolium. 'What a precious thing this fine old berberis is, . . . individually one of the handsomest of small shrubs, it is at its very best in mid-winter, every leaf is a marvel of beautiful drawing and construction . . . in spring the whole picture changes—the polished leaves are green again . . . it is the only hardy shrub I can think of that is in one or other of its varied forms of beauty throughout the year' (pp. 21–22).
Carnation. '. . . the flower that has the firmest hold on the gardener's heart' (p. 94).
Ceanothus. ' "*Gloire de Versailles*", my favourite of its kind' (pp. 22, 205).
Chimonanthus fragrans (praecox). 'One of the sweetest and strongest scented of the year's blooms . . .' (p. 229).

---

[1] *Home and Garden*, p. 27.   [2] Ibid., p. 58.
[3] *Colour Schemes for the Flower Garden*, p. 135.

Clematis davidiana. 'Spreading masses of the beautiful C.D. . . . and flowers of a pale-blue colour of a delicate and uncommon quality' (pp. 95, 205).

Clematis flammula. '. . . this lovely and tender-scented clematis . . .' (p. 25).

Corydalis capnoides. 'Is a charming rock plant, with flowers of palest sulphur colour, one of the neatest and most graceful of its family' (p. 50).

Cowslip. 'All the scented flowers of the primrose tribe are delightful . . . the actual sweetness is most apparent in the cowslip' (p. 230).

Daffodil. 'But the glory of the copse just now consists in the great stretches of daffodils' (p. 48).

Delphinium belladonna. '. . . had so lovely a quality of colour that it is quite indispensable' (p. 91).

Dog-tooth violet. 'What a charm there is about the Dog-tooth violet; it is pretty everywhere, in borders, in the rock-garden, in all sorts of corners' (p. 33).

Elder tree. 'I am very fond of the elder-tree. It is a sociable sort of thing . . .' (p. 83).

Eryngium oliverianum. '. . . has an admirable structure . . . equalling it in beauty is *E. giganteum* . . .' (p. 93).

Funkia grandiflora (Hosta plantaginea). '. . . whose fresh-looking pale green leaves are delightful . . .' (p. 212).

Geranium. (pelargonium) '. . . . I love geraniums . . . I love their strangely pleasant smell, and their beautiful modern colourings of soft scarlet and salmon-scarlet and salmon-pink . . .' (p. 267).

Grape vine (Royal Muscadine). 'The best of all climbing or rambling plants . . .' (p. 42).

Guelder rose. (*Vibernum opulus*) '. . . is beautiful anywhere, but I think it best of all on the cold side of a wall' (p. 71).

Gypsophila paniculata '. . . is one of the most useful plants . . . its delicate masses of bloom are like clouds of flowery mist settled down upon the flower borders' (p. 95).

Hartstongue fern (*Phyllitis scolopendrium*). 'Farther along the Hartstongue gives way to *Iris foetidissima* . . . nothing to my mind looks better than these two plants at the base of a wall on the cool side' (p. 120).

Hollyhock. 'By far the most beautiful is one of a pure pink colour, with a wide outer frill. It came first from a cottage garden, and has always since been treasured' (p. 105).

Iris graminea. '. . . of all irises I know, the sweetest to smell is a later blooming one, *I. graminea*' (p. 229).

Iris reticulata. 'No flower of the whole year can show a more splendid and sumptuous colour than the purple of *I. reticulata*' (p. 33).

Iris stylosa (*unguicularis*). 'I never tire of admiring and praising *Iris stylosa*, which has proved itself such a good plant for English gardens; at any rate, for those in our southern counties. Lovely in form and colour, sweetly scented and with admirable foliage, it has in addition to these merits, the unusual one of a blooming season of six months' (p. 13).

Jasmine. '. . . the ever-delightful white Jasmine . . .' (p. 43).

Juniper. 'One of the best shrubs either for garden or wild . . . a colouring as delicately subtle in its own way as that of cloud or mist . . . the stems of the twigs are of a warm, almost foxy colour . . . wonderfully delicate . . . intangible quality of colouring . . . throughout the winter the rugged-barked stems are clothed with loveliest pale green growths of a silvery quality' (p. 31).

Kalmia. 'The beauty of the flower was always an unending delight'.[1]

Lavender. 'To reap its fragrant harvest is one of the many joys of the flower year' (p. 105).

Lent hellebore. '. . . beautiful late-flowering' (p. 57).

Leycesteria formosa. '. . . is a soft-wooded shrub, whose beauty, without being showy, is full of charm and refinement' (p. 100).

Lilac. 'The white variety, Marie Legraye, always remains my favourite . . . Among the many beautiful coloured lilacs, I am fond of Lucie Baltet and Princess Marie' (p. 23).

Lilium auratum, harrisi, speciosum, giganteum.

London Pride. '. . . which I think quite the most beautiful of the saxifrages of this section. . . . When its pink cloud of bloom is at its best, I always think it the prettiest thing in the garden' (p. 120).

Love-in-a-Mist. 'A plant I hold in high admiration' (p. 251).

Magnolia—*soulangiana, denudata* (*conspicua*), *liliflora* (*purpurea*), *stellata*. 'I had . . . a large clump for just the things I like best . . . these are mostly junipers and magnolias . . .' (p. 101).

Marsh marigold (*Caltha palustris*). 'Marshy hollows in the valleys are brilliant with marsh marigold . . .' (p. 52).

Meconopsis napaulensis wallichii. 'Every winter I notice how lovely the pale woolly foliage of this plant bears up against the early winter's frost and wet' (p. 165).

[1] This is included from *Children and Gardens*, p. 53, as it was a special favourite.

Megasea (*Bergenia*) *cordifolia*. 'I am never tired of admiring the fine solid foliage of this family of plants, remaining, as it does, in beauty both winter and summer, and taking on a splendid winter colouring of warm red bronze.'

Myrtle. 'The wild bog-myrtle so common in Scotland has almost the sweetness of true myrtle . . .' (p. 238).

Nandina domestica. 'The Chinese plant it for good luck near their houses. If it is as lucky as it is pretty, it ought to do one good . . . it struck me as one of the most beautiful growing things I have ever seen . . .' (p. 206).

Nemophila. 'A single plant will often cover a square yard with its beautiful blue bloom . . .' (p. 113).

Night-scented stock. 'But of all the family, the finest fragrance comes from the small annual night-scented stock . . .' (p. 239).

Paeony (tree, China, etc.). List of 26 (p. 74).

Phacelia campanulata '. . . a splendid gentian-blue . . .' (p. 63).

Polypody fern. 'One of the best of cool wall plants . . .' (p. 121).

Primrose. 'One year, thinking it might be useful to classify them, I tried to do so, but gave it up after writing out the characters of sixty classes!' (p. 217).

Quince. 'How seldom does one see quinces planted for ornament, and yet there is hardly any small tree that better deserves such treatment.'

Rhododendron. '. . . varieties beautiful in themselves' (p. 64).

Rose—Sweetbriars (Lord Penzance). 'The whole garden is fragrant with sweetbriar' (p. 51).

    Dundee rambler and Garland rose. 'That excellent old rose, the Dundee rambler, or the still prettier Garland rose . . .' (p. 39).

    Fortune's yellow. 'The flowers have such incomparable beauty' (p. 41).

    Madame Alfred Carrière. 'Two other roses of free growth are also favourites' (p. 80).

        (See her book *Roses for the English Garden*.)

St Helena Violet. '. . . delicate colouring' (p. 45).

Satin-leaf (*Heuchera richardsonii*). 'The beauty of the plant is in the colour and texture of the foliage' (p. 53).

Snapdragon. '. . . of the older type. These I always think one of the best and most interesting and admirable of garden plants' (p. 251).

Sweet gale (Myrica). '. . . . crushed leaves give a grateful fragrance' (p. 34).

Trillium. 'Little jewels of beauty' (p. 270).

Tulip. *Tulipa retroflexa*, Couleur de Vin, Bleu Céleste, etc. 'The great garden flowers in the last week of April and the earliest days of May' (p. 55).

Wallflower. 'The sweetness of a sun-baked bank of wallflower belongs to April' (p. 230).

White everlasting pea. 'Nothing in the garden has been more useful than a hedge of the white everlasting pea' (p. 95).

Woodruff. 'What scent is so delicate as that of its leaves?' (p. 60).

Wood violet. 'It seems to me to be quite the best of all the violet scents' (p. 231).

Yucca. 'They are good to look at all times of the year' (p. 91).

Zinnia. '. . . another fine annual' (p. 251).

Having listed most of her favourite flowers, it is now absolutely essential to mention some of her 'ugly ducklings'. There is a Hans Andersen touch about her reference to a malformed fruit or flower, and almost any plant which, for some reason or another suffers unpopularity, may at once depend on her support. She could always point out that it was not the fault of the plant, but that either it had been placed inartistically, or its whole growth had not been appreciated 'She speaks as tenderly of a deformed pear as she might of some crippled child. "One is so sorry", she says, "for a poor fruit".'[1]

Perhaps it is this appreciation of the plant as a whole, or its proper situation, which may explain her defence of aucuba, the golden privet, the laurel and the sweet bay. Much maligned as are the first three, it is instructive to read her notes about each of them. Grown naturally, using the best material from each, they have their uses and their attraction. The aucuba, if not allowed to become straggly and dirty, can have 'bright green leaves glistening with abundant health and vigour' if planted 'the furthest possible in sentiment from the fussy unrest of the roadside shrubbery, enduring as well as it may the endless showerings of chimney-blacks and smotherings or road-dust'.[2] The golden privet has only to be seen growing into a free-branching shrub and not clipped back tightly into a hedge to be appreciated for its effect of streaming sunlight. Miss Jekyll includes it in her flower border. 'Its clean, cheerful, bright yellow gives a note of just the right colour all through the summer.'[3] Then comes her defence of the laurel.

'The common laurel is generally seen as a long-suffering garden hack. . . . Planted in thin woodland and never pruned, it grows into

---

[1] *Children and Gardens*, p. 56.   [2] *Flower Decoration in the House*, p.2.
[3] *Colour Schemes for the Garden*, pp. 68 and 146.

a small tree that takes curious ways and shapes of trunk and branch of character that is remarkably pictorial.' Perhaps the sweet bay does not need defending quite so much. Its culinary value is of course unquestionable, but one has to study its growth carefully to appreciate Miss Jekyll's warmth of feeling for it. 'Of all the lovely forms of branch and leaf, the one that may be said to be of supremest beauty— that of the sweet bay—. . . the whole structure showing the most admirable design for strength and beauty . . . is a truly a thing to marvel at. . . .'[1]

Perhaps her most startling appreciation comes in her defence of the three Victorian 'horrors' of the bedding-out system. There are people, she says, who will not now 'admit scarlet geranium, or blue lobelia, or yellow calceolaria' into their gardens. 'But,' she goes on, 'properly employed, these are all good garden plants, and it was not their fault that they were used in uninteresting ways.'[2] (In another of her books she describes some of these 'uninteresting ways' in rather stronger terms— 'Its worst form of all was the "ribbon border", generally a line of scarlet geranium at the back, then a line of calceolaria, then a line of blue lobelia . . . and lastly a line of the inevitable golden Feather Feverfew . . . could anything be more tedious or more stupid ?')[3]

In her book *Colour Schemes for the Flower Garden*, she mentions two or three times in various borders the use of the 'lower-growing plants of purest blue', lobelia 'cobalt blue' and the taller *Lobelia tenuior* and the 'thin drifts of the pale canary-yellow *Calceolaria amplexicaulis*'.

She uses the cobalt blue of the lobelia, not the Oxford blue, and the clear primrose yellow of the calceolaria, not the deep custard colour. She plants them, not next to vivid splashes of colour in straight lines like soldiers, but in clumps or 'drifts', next to variegated mint, longiflorum lilies, lemon-and-white snapdragons in the case of the calceolaria, and the lobelia against a very pale pink penstemon 'Spitzberg', among grey foliage of santolina and *Stachys lanata*.

When she says 'properly employed these are all good garden plants' she is stating the fundamental fact of all flowers. Like people—if studied with understanding, they will appear to their best advantage.

The following dialogue, although fictitious, illustrates the misconception that prevailed in some people's minds in this matter.

'"My grandfather had a few roses," said Richard, "but geraniums, calceolarias and lobelias were his staple. Those were the regular flowers of a gentleman's villa garden at that time, before Miss Jekyll

---

[1] *Flower Decoration in the House*, p. 8.   [2] *Colour Planning of the Garden*, Introduction.
[3] *Wood and Garden*, p. 266.

had got to work with her revolutionary beautifying hand. No one person can so have transformed the face of England as the Lady of Munstead. . . ."

' "We had a rich neighbour with a garden just like your grandfather's," said Jenny. "A bookmaker. Was your grandfather a bookmaker?"

' "No such luck," said Richard.

' "He was away during the week," said Jenny, "but on Sundays he was always at home and there were noisy friends in dog-carts and wagonettes and even four-in-hands, all with big watchchains and rings and cigars. They wouldn't have enjoyed it half so much if there had been no geraniums."

' "More people like geraniums than not," said Richard. "Miss Jekyll, while she was making England more lovely, was depriving many a simple soul of scarlet comfort." '[1]

According to Richard, one would have a picture of Miss Jekyll sweeping through the countryside, ordering the instant dismissal of all geraniums and other brightly coloured bedding plants from every garden. In her own words she defends the geraniums, but condemns the way in which they are used: '. . . Not once but many a time my visitors have expressed unbounded surprise when they saw these plants in my garden, saying, "I should have thought that you would have despised geraniums". On the contrary, I love geraniums. There are no plants to come near them for pot, or box, or stone basket, or for massing in any sheltered place in hottest sunshine; and I love their strangely pleasant smell, and their beautiful modern colourings of soft scarlet and salmon-scarlet and salmon-pink . . . . In the case of my visitors, when they have expressed surprise at my having "those horrid old bedding plants" in my garden, it seemed quite a new view when I pointed out that bedding plants were only passive agents in their own misuse, and that a geranium was a geranium long before it was a bedding plant!'[2]

This is her own defence, but the Editor of *Gardening Illustrated* many years later took up the cudgels on her behalf.

'It has been said . . . that Miss Jekyll was responsible for sweeping away the old system of bedding out, ribbon borders, and carpet bedding, but this is not true. Miss Jekyll was not the kind of gardener to boast of not having a geranium in her garden. She grew many varieties of bedding geraniums or pelargoniums, also begonias, calceolarias and lobelias, but her plants were always used in congenial surroundings and with good colour effect.

[1] *The Barber's Clock.*   [2] *Wood and Garden*, pp. 267–8.

'Above all, Miss Jekyll was broad-minded. She was not opposed to topiary work if it fitted into the picture. Miss Jekyll was fond of cats, and two yew trees on the lawn at Munstead which of themselves took the form suggesting a cat were clipped to form a large comfortable-looking yew cat, to which no one could possibly take exception.'

CHAPTER XIV

1922–1932

The last ten years—Her influence on gardens and gardening—
Gardens remaining today which show her ideas—
Her life's work in her books

———————

Her portrait had been exhibited in the Grafton Gallery and whatever
she had felt about the painting of it, she appreciated it as a work of art,
especially the portrait of her gardening boots. She would not have cared
for publicity any more than her dear friend Brabby cared for it, but
there must have been a certain satisfaction in the fact that her portrait
was of importance to other people on account of her work, as well as
on account of its value as a painting. In 1922 there was another mark of
appreciation for her work from the gardening world—the award of
the Veitch Memorial Gold Medal. (See Curtis's *Botanical Magazine*,
'Dedications and Portraits', 1827–1927.)

Garden Ornament, her latest book, shows an interesting development
in ideas and taste and especially the influence of Lutyens on her work
as, in their earlier collaboration, one could see her influence on his.
Her increased interest in the architect's part of a garden is obvious and
she is also ready to accept a more formal design if it fits into her picture.
At one time such a design would have been discarded without further
thought. It is pleasant to know that they were still in close touch after
so many years, while he himself was going from strength to strength
with plans and designs tumbling one after another, with many considerable commissions in this country, and with the magnificence of
Delhi taking shape at the other side of the world. Miss Jekyll was, of
course, consulted about planting designs and had a note 'small trees
for the Delhi model'. At home Lutyens had been working on plans
which included Britannic House, Finsbury Circus (1920), the Midland
Bank, Piccadilly (1922) and Gledstone Hall, Yorkshire (1923).

Gledstone Hall, between Skipton and Gisburn, had many interesting
features, especially a fine architecturally planned sunk garden. Mr

Hussey writes: '. . . the garden structure, supporting a distant prospect, is softened by a Jekyll planting scheme.'[1]

'There is no better example of the collaboration between Sir Edwin Lutyens and Gertrude Jekyll; of the combination of architectural form with impressionist planting. The formal element perhaps predominates more here than in the masterpiece of Lutyens–Jekyll design—the garden at Hestercombe, Somerset. For clothing of a stone frame with vegetation Miss Jekyll was very fond of *Megasea cordifolia*—at Hestercombe its strong leathery leaves, so unexpectedly equipped with fat pink cowslip flowers in February, frame a whole vast parterre. Here it is prominent in strategic positions, in company with the larger-leaved saxifrages, *Senecio clivorum*, *Acanthus mollis*, *Rodgersia*, and red-hot pokers.'[2]

This was in 1923, Miss Jekyll's eightieth year. Writing to a friend at this time she apologises for not being able to see many visitors, but there was still work to be done and she was still ready to do it, especially when it meant working with Lutyens. The next project was the Queen's Dolls' House, for which she designed the garden. Sir Edwin Lutyens was the architect—'He builds a New Delhi, eighty square miles of palace and avenue; he builds a Queen's Dolls' House, an affair of inches but such that Japanese cherry stone carvers could not excel'[3] —and in his file referring to this unusual commission is a letter from Miss Jekyll dated 17th March, 1923, 'asking about the colouring, and exact proportion of the upper moulding, of garden pots—one inch high!— with the potter's attempts at which she was not satisfied'. This was characteristically painstaking on Miss Jekyll's side and on Lutyens' side there was the characteristic joking as is illustrated by the story of the embroidered pillowslips—M.G. on one and G.M. on the other. Why were the initials changed round, Queen Mary wished to know. 'For "May George?" ma'am, and "George May!" came Sir Edwin's quick reply.'

In 1924 she suffered a personal loss. One of the drawbacks of living to an old age is that so often one's family and contemporaries have died; Horace Walpole expresses it, 'a heavy calamity—the surviving of one's friends'. Miss Jekyll was fortunate in still having some of her family alive. Mrs Eden, her sister Carry, who had lived most of her life in Venice and had returned to England latterly, was approaching ninety and her younger brother Walter, who had come on some of the Chalet parties years ago in Switzerland, was still alive as also her

---

[1] *Life of Sir Edwin Lutyens.*   [2] *Country Life*, 13th and 20th April, 1935.
[3] *The Book of the Queen's Dolls' House*, by E. V. Lucas. Methuen, 1924.

favourite brother, Sir Herbert Jekyll. But this was a friend, and friends with whom she felt at ease, as one does as one gets older only with long-standing friendships, were becoming scarce.

This friend who died was Mr James Britten, whom Miss Jekyll must have sadly missed, for she had got to know him well in these later years. Mr Pearsall Smith commented: 'I was an assiduous reader of dictionaries; on English dialects Britten was an expert; Gertrude Jekyll knew a lot about them also, and our discussions on these subjects were often full of delight and disagreement.'[1] (Mr Britten had, in fact, written a book for The English Dialect Society, *Old Country and Farming Words*, published in 1880. This was exactly the kind of subject to appeal to Miss Jekyll.)

During 1924 Miss Jekyll was revising the script of *Old West Surrey*. It was to be substantially enlarged and to have many more photographs, and the labour involved must have been considerable. The result was published in 1925 as *Old English Household Life* and gives some idea of her encyclopaedic knowledge and her collections, now housed in the Surrey Archeological Museum at Guildford. A gracious comment comes from Sir Edwin Lutyens writing in a number of *English Life*: 'It has been a matter of profound satisfaction for me to have been able here to pay even a passing tribute to this book [*Old English Household Life*] and to its author: not that I flatter myself I have thus discharged even in the smallest degree any of my great obligation to Miss Jekyll, her wisdom and encouragement, which has accumulated now over many years.'

It is difficult to understand how she could still get through so much work—her doctor at this period had prescribed one day of every week to be spent in bed, which must have cut short the valuable time for work alarmingly. A postcard dated 15th May, 1925, to the Viscountess Wolseley explains that she was less able to be at the disposal of visitors. 'Your friend, and theirs, will be very welcome on or near 22nd May. Will they kindly give me what notice they can of the day—from any time after 3.30 afternoons. I am obliged to have a complete rest in the earlier afternoon.' (signed G. Jekyll) (This was the daughter of the previous Lady Wolseley, who had died in 1920, and the Founder of the Glynde School for Lady Gardeners, of which Miss Jekyll, Mrs C. W. Earle and Miss Willmott were Patrons.)

Miss Jekyll still took up her paintbrush sometimes and was delighted when, in 1926, Mr Musgrave, of the R.H.S., invited her to paint a sign for the White Horse at Hascombe. Miss Musgrave, who has the

[1] *Reperusals and Recollections*, L. Pearsall Smith. Constable.

163

original painting in her care, told me that the sign remained in position until about eleven years ago. Miss Jekyll's prancing white horse with flowing mane and tail has now been replaced by a more sedate and placid animal standing quietly against a stretch of blue sky. Her interest in local matters was always alive and she liked especially to do things for her own village or for Godalming, the nearest town. (She had designed the garden for Godalming Police Station, and kept up almost to the end of her life her attendance at the Godalming branch committee meetings of the National Trust).

Articles were still being contributed to *English Life*, the *Empire Review* and the *Gardener's Chronicle*, and précis of her ideas on colour schemes for the garden went into the Introduction of a book, *Colour Planning of the Garden*, by G. F. Tilney, T. Humphreys and W. Irving. A revised edition of *Garden Ornament*, with Christopher Hussey, came out in 1927 which must have entailed more writing and editing, as the Foreword mentions that 'fresh sections have been inserted . . . and old ones have been pruned and supplemented'. In 1928, at the age of eighty-five, she had an article in *The Nineteenth Century* on 'The Changes of Fashion in Gardening'.

Two more family losses came about this time. In December, 1928, her sister Carry died at the age of ninety-one, and a few months afterwards her brother Walter died in Jamaica, aged eighty.

In 1928 Ned Lutyens had completed plans for the Westminster Housing Scheme and, two years earlier, for Grosvenor House and The Embassy, Washington. In 1930 came another highlight in his career. He had always longed to build a cathedral or some great building to the glory of God. A friend has recalled an earlier occasion when Ned Lutyens was pacing up and down the room in his usual excited way, saying to Miss Jekyll: 'Aunt Gertrude, I want to build palaces and cathedrals', to which she replied: Ned, you can't *begin* by being buried in Westminster Abbey.' 'Oh, but I have!,' he replied, and then went on to tell the story of a visit to the dentist for an extraction. Afterwards, it happened that he was wandering along near the Abbey, with the tooth rolling about in his pocket. What does one do with an old tooth? He fingered it and felt it and then, in a typical Lutyens moment, walked into the Abbey and dropped it down a grid in the central heating. And so he declared that at least his tooth was buried in Westminster Abbey. After the success of Delhi and the achievements of the last twenty years it was not surprising that when the Archbishop of Liverpool wanted to found a Roman Catholic church second only to St Peter's, Lutyens should be approached. The

English cathedral had been designed by a Roman Catholic. Why shouldn't the Roman Catholic one be designed by a member of the Church of England?

'*Au fond* I am horribly religious, but cannot speak of it and this saves my work.' This is how he wrote to a friend when he was a young man, and the plans for this cathedral meant so much to him that, as usual, a certain amount of levity had to come into the proceedings. He was delighted when the first words of the Archbishop on the occasion of their meeting for discussion of plans were: 'Will you have a cocktail?' Another first introduction, this time to Father Ronald Knox, opened with his query: ' "Do you know it is a scientific fact that when you cut a carrot its temperature drops?" Father Knox was quite equal to the occasion. He replied: "Yes, and when you cut a friend his temperature rises!" '[1]

And so the designs for the Cathedral of Christ the King, Liverpool, went forward and no one was surprised or shocked when, in serious conference, a clockwork mouse was loosed over the plans. The project was of such magnitude that sometimes it had to be treated lightly.

While these larger commissions were filling Lutyens' timetable, Miss Jekyll's interests, though still centring on her garden, were developing in another direction. She had always been interested in the use of words—Mr Falkner related that 'among her minor interests was a love of precision in the use of the English language in which she herself had a slightly Victorian prejudice', and gave an instance of her exactitude in the advice of words. Some nurserymen had introduced a strain of zinnia which they called '*robustus elegans*'. She insisted that these terms were contradictory. 'For instance', Miss Jekyll explained, 'I should call you *robustus* but I should not call you *elegans*'. This was a cool piece of repartee as, at the time, Miss Jekyll probably weighed some fourteen stone herself and he probably about eleven.

This interest in the use of the English language was of perhaps greater value and comfort to her now than ever before. She had always delighted in a good-natured battle of words. These had been fought with skill and a certain amount of cunning against Mr Britten and Mr Pearsall Smith. Now that Mr Britten had died, the last few years of her life were greatly enlivened by the arguments she was still able to enjoy with Mr Pearsall Smith. On his leaving Haslemere for Oxford some years previously, they had kept up a correspondence of post cards and letters. Through Britten Mr Pearsall Smith had been introduced to Robert Bridges whom he joined on the committee of the Society

[1] *The Life of Sir Edwin Lutyens.*

for Pure English. When he wrote pamphlets for the S.P.E. under the stern eye of Bridges, he sent copies to Miss Jekyll for her comment and 'always received in answer a prompt and cordial note of appreciation and thanks'. They had kept in touch through this common interest as collectors keep in touch. In this case the collection was not of coins or porcelain, stamps or early watches, but words.

Miss Jekyll, nearly blind, was approaching ninety when Mr Pearsall Smith appeared once more on her horizon, living again in Surrey after many years near Oxford. He was one of the few visitors she was now able to enjoy, and he describes his first visit to Munstead Wood after such a long absence.

He had been to see Sir Herbert Jekyll at Munstead House and was conducted from there across the country road to the small door in Miss Jekyll's enclosing fence of spiles. It was locked, but the key hung on a hidden nail and he writes of the feeling of entering a secret garden through the gateway in the wooden fencing. (The door is still there and the pathway inside leads through a quiet area of woodland to the wider grass paths between banks of rhododendrons and shrubs to the stretch of lawn in front of the house.)

Miss Jekyll was ready to receive her visitor with a list of words prepared beforehand. He thought she might have altered greatly in her old age and did not want to tire her or exploit her weakness. 'Weakness! Miss Jekyll was as ready as ever for a scrap, and it was impossible, or almost impossible, when she held a view strongly, to make her give way an inch.'[1]

She was greatly interested in the use of local words and in particular the derivation of the word 'tiller'. 'They use it about here to describe the shoots and suckers that grow from the stump of a tree they've cut down; is it the same word as the tiller of a boat, or is it a different word? You don't know? Do, please, look it up, will you, and send me a post card?'[2]

After consulting the Oxford Dictionary, Mr Pearsall Smith recalls sending her the details of the derivation of 'tiller'—that it is an old word brought by the Teutons to England and found in an Anglo-Saxon translation of Genesis, but not found again until used by John Evelyn. The meanings given are: 'shoot of plant springing from bottom of original stalk; sapling; sucker'. The word tiller in connection with a boat is derived from quite a different source—from the medieval Latin *telarium* meaning a weaver's beam.

One of their best arguments described by Mr Pearsall Smith was

[1] *Reperusals and Recollections.* Constable.   [2] Ibid.

on the use and distinction of the words 'ride' and 'drive'. Miss Jekyll sat in her accustomed chair, '. . . her eyes still twinkled behind her heavy glasses, the sound of her deep chuckle was quite as rich as ever'. She declared that 'ride' was only used when riding on a horse or donkey or camel, something with four legs, or something analogous like a bicycle. Mr Pearsall Smith contended that 'drive' was used for riding in or on something under one's control, and 'ride' for a vehicle driven by someone else, like a bus or carriage.

'"But, Miss Jekyll, if you go on a bus, don't you take a 'ride' on it?"'

'"But I never go on a bus!" she triumphed.'

'"But if you were given a lift by a farmer on the road?"'

'"I should call it a lift; a lift, certainly, not a 'ride'."'

'"But suppose, Miss Jekyll, that you wanted to go home from a hay-field on a loaded haycart? Wouldn't you ask if you could have a 'ride' on the cart? Wouldn't you have to say 'ride'—not 'drive'?"'

'Miss Jekyll looked disconcerted. "Well", she said at last, "no, I shouldn't call it a 'drive'. No, certainly not a 'drive'".'

'"Would you ask for a lift, then?"'

'"No, I shouldn't call it a 'lift'."'

'"Now, Miss Jekyll", I insisted (for the spirit of pedantry, a spirit that spares neither age nor sex, had taken possession of me), "now, honestly, what would you ask for?"'

'Miss Jekyll seemed almost to sweat blood at this question.

'"I should ask—well, I should ask—if you will insist on knowing— I suppose I should ask for a 'ride' on the haycart. But", she added, with what was almost a wicked wink from behind her spectacles, "but then, you know, I should be speaking to quite uneducated people."'

'This wasn't fair; she knew it wasn't fair, and her wink betrayed her.'

But Miss Jekyll was not to be so easily defeated. The next visit from Mr Pearsall Smith provided her with an opportunity for her victory. She was fully prepared, when he arrived, for a brisk encounter. Part of her success in these battles was to lull her opponent into a feeling of false security by appealing to their 'greater knowledge'. These tactics even misled such an experienced combatant as Mr Pearsall Smith and on this particular occasion he remarks that he was nicely taken in.

'. . . mildly, almost deferentially, she said: "There is a word whose derivation I want you to tell me."

' "What is it?" I incautiously asked.

' "It is the word," she said, "*epergne*. You know what an *epergne* is, a big centre dish for the dinner table, with branches. But why is it called *epergne*? What is the word derived from?"

' "It's a French word", I answered.

' "No, it isn't," she snapped. "There's no such word in French. They call it a *surtout*. I thought that you could explain it for me."

'She knew, I suspect, that I couldn't explain *epergne* as no one knows its source and derivation.

' "You can't explain *epergne*!" she exclaimed with vigour, as though it were an *epergne* itself she was hurling at me. Then she grunted with delight, and her discomfiture on the haycart was avenged and forgotten.'

Her triumph with the *epergne* was not forgotten, however, and it was repeated with pride and joy to her old friend Sir Edwin Lutyens. (There is a note in *English Domestic Silver* which throws some light on this matter: 'The elaborate epergnes of the eighteenth century took on the dinner table the place of honour which had been relinquished by the great salt. They were designed to save (épargner) the trouble of passing things at table, but the word, despite its French appearance, is Anglo-Gallic and probably could not be found before 1700'.)[1]

Mr Pearsall Smith recalls that he sometimes introduced again the subject of gardening, with which, when he was a younger man, she often helped and encouraged him. However, this was not a success on these later meetings; 'a veil of fatigue, of boredom with all the garden chatter of the world, seemed to dim her face' as she looked at him from behind her heavy glasses. There might be a small pause. Immediately she was ready to rush into another word argument, having dismissed the subject of her life's work almost in a split second.

Then there was the list of Miss Jekyll's quality words.

With all respect to Miss Nancy Mitford and Professor Ross the word which Miss Jekyll selected to describe her list of 'quality words' seems to be superior to the use of 'U' and 'non-U' in derivation and also in sound. Miss Jekyll revived the old word 'armigerous', whose meaning 'entitled to bear arms' has a genuine connection with the whole matter, The word 'armiger' is often seen on tombstones in old churchyards, used rather as the original meaning for gentleman or squire. The engraving may read: 'In beloved memory of So-and-So, armiger.'

Discussing this with Mr Pearsall Smith, Miss Jekyll explained: 'armigerous people have certain expressions of their own. They don't, for instance, say overcoat—that's an Americanism—but greatcoat; they have tea or coffee or sugar, they never take them; they never take anything into their bodies but pills and medicines, and these they don't talk about. . . .'

[1] *English Domestic Silver*, Charles Oman, p. 114.

Miss Jekyll went on to enumerate further terms of convention, and the conversation ended on the usual slightly teasing note of good humour, with each trying to get a rise out of the other.

'Now, Miss Jekyll', Mr Pearsall Smith records their final talk together, taking his leave after only a short visit in case of tiring her too much, 'now that you have told me of these nice discriminations, what would you advise a non-armigerous person to say or do? Would you advise me to keep to the usages of my own condition?'

'We stood at the open door; Miss Jekyll looked at me with her plain but splendid face—and her friendliness seemed to be struggling with an unregenerate impulse derived from the first of lady-gardeners; she snorted, she almost winked and then she chuckled. "Well, I think if I were you—yes", she went on after another pause of serious considera-tion in which she eyed me from head to foot, "Yes, I think, if you insist upon an answer, yes—you had better stick to the ways of your class."

'With this parting shot which the old Amazon delivered from her bow with undiminished vigour at the age of eighty-eight, Miss Jekyll laughed her jolly laugh, in which I could not help joining as I took my leave.'

But the last note to be struck was a garden one.

' "Go and have a look at the gardens if you like", she added, "and there's a big patch of blue meconopsis behind the tool-shed you might like to see. I'm sorry I can't come and show it to you. Goodbye, and come to see me again soon." '[1]

This last session on words must have taken place in the early summer of 1932. She was eighty-eight and the meconopsis were making a good show, but she was not able to take Mr Pearsall Smith to see them herself. In fact, during this summer her progress round her garden was made in an invalid chair, a method which she resented to some extent, but it made it possible for her to see how things were going and to keep up her interest in her plants and flowers. This chair was Lutyens' gift to her.

It is gratifying to know that at least she was well enough to enjoy her last summer in the garden which she had made, although it was usually from the confines of a wheeled chair. Perhaps she was able, even more than ever before, to take from her garden that refreshment and 'ease to the mind' of which she so often wrote: 'A garden . . . gives the delightful feeling of repose, and refreshment, and purest enjoyment of beauty, that seems to be the best fulfillment of its purpose. . . .'[2]

But this was no sentimental viewpoint. She also wrote: 'There is no

---

[1] *Reperusals and Recollections.* Constable   [2] *Wood and Garden*, p. 2.

royal road. It is no use asking me or anyone else how to dig . . . better go and watch a man digging, and then take a spade and try to do it. . . .'[1] But after the hard labour, the disappointments, frustrations and failures, which she warns the prospective gardener to expect, there will come 'the enduring happiness that the love of a garden gives. . .'[2]

Her work was still going forward. Precious seeds were collected from the garden, among them *Meconopsis baileyi* (*M. betonicifolia*), and articles were written for the series she was sending in for the Bramley Parish magazine on Recollections of Old Bramley. Notes and articles were still being sent in for *Gardening Illustrated* and a new edition of *Wall and Water Gardens* was being prepared.

Her personal correspondence was also kept up, an example of which was a letter to Mrs E. V. Clark of Street, Somerset.

Munstead Wood,
Godalming.

August 26, 1932.
Dear Mrs Clark,

I am so sorry that so many days have passed since I had your kind letter and the photographs of your garden, but I now thank you sincerely for both. The delay is because of my infirmities—my years are 88 and there are times when my doctor keeps me very close on account of a worn-out heart, so that many things that I ought to do have to be set aside.

I am thankful that my books have been of use to you. If they have any merit it is because I have never written a word that was not a record of work actually done and because I had some early training in the fine arts.

yrs gratefully,
G. Jekyll.

It almost seemed as though her reserves of strength might carry her through the next winter, but towards the end of September there came a severe blow—the sudden death of Herbert Jekyll, the brother who was closest to her of all the family and who had lived near at hand for so many years. At her age and in her state of health this was probably a decisive factor.

On 29th November she celebrated her eighty-ninth birthday, and on 8th December—about a fortnight later, after quite a short illness—she died peacefully.

If one is a gardener there is something to be said for dying with the dying year. In December, when the last of the roses are clinging bravely

[1] *Wood and Garden.* p. 189.   [2] *Wood and Garden.*

to the skeleton stems and the shining leaves of the evergreens are coming into their own, there is a feeling of rest from labour, a time of preparation, a storing up of energy and a respite from toil and exertion. The silent earth and the bare trees sleep and while they sleep a new building up process is quietly at work, unseen and unheard.

Gertrude Jekyll had worked long and energetically throughout her life in the face of difficulties and now, when the plants and flowers and trees which she knew and loved so well were taking their rest, in preparation for a new life, she was taking hers. The store of her wisdom and knowledge was safely packed away in her books, the harvest of her experience gathered in. It seemed as though she was one with nature inasmuch as the calendar of the year was also hers. Her wisdom had come to her through the brightness and hope of spring, through the joy of summer and the beauty of autumn, and finally through her belief in the miracle of new life after the winter.

She was buried on 12th December at the church of St John the Baptist, Busbridge. Some of the items for the service she had chosen herself years beforehand. Most of it, as might be expected, expressed thanksgiving and trust: Psalm CIII: 'Praise the Lord, O my soul: and all that is within me praise His holy Name,' and the lesson from the Revelation of St John the Divine, XXI. 1–7: 'And I saw a new heaven and a new earth: for the first heaven and the first earth were passed away: and there was no more sea.' The organ was played by Pamela McKenna—the girl for whom the cats' tea-party had been held many years earlier. The chorale by Bach, *Commit thy way to Jesus*, and the hymn *Abide with me* were sung. She had particularly requested the playing of Handel's *Largo*—she used to say it was her prayer— and the *Nunc Dimittis* was sung at the grave.

A letter from Miss Willmott written to Mr Cowley at the time of her death expresses affection and appreciation:

> Warley Place,
> Great Warley,
> Essex.

Dear Mr Cowley,

I have just had a telegram from Lady Jekyll with the sad tidings of Miss Jekyll's death. I am sure it will grieve you deeply and I am full of sorrow at the loss of one I admired so greatly and loved sincerely. She was such a sensitive and great personality. I so thoroughly realised it, perhaps more than others.

In her were all the qualities I most admire, for apart from being a great gardener and lover of plants, her sense of beauty and the picturesque in a garden combined with horticulture and cultivation at its best is very rarely found. In fact I have never known it except in my sister Mrs Berkeley of Spetchley.

It was always a matter of surprise to me that the many activities and her different material and artistic achievements were all of the best and highest. I was 15 when I first knew her. Then the awe she inspired in me in the course of years became admiration and affection. You who knew her so well had so many opportunities of knowing her great attainments. I saw her last in August just before I was taken ill with bronchial pneumonia. It was a great effort to go to Munstead but I had a feeling I must go. Her last letter was upon Sir Herbert's death. On the occasion of my last visit she mentioned that the notes I made about her and which you published had given her more pleasure than anything else written about her. I gave an evening about her at the Garden Club with slides of views in her garden. Several of her family were present and they all seemed pleased.

Although the present generation of so-called gardeners knew her only as a name, to all of us who knew her she was always a living force, an example and an inspiration.

It was Sir Herbert's death which must have hastened her death for her last letter to me was very pathetic.

Perhaps I may see you at the R.H.S. on Tuesday.

Yours faithfully,

Dec. 9.   E. Willmott.

Looking back over these ninety years it seems almost impossible that so many changes could take place in so short a time. The introduction of gas, electricity, anaesthetics, motor cars, bicycles, aeroplanes and wireless sets, sewing machines and gramophones, railways and tarmacadam roads—to mention only some of them—were among the contributors to an altered way of life in one woman's span of years.

Gertrude Jekyll was the kind of person who would, one feels sure, have lived according to her own rule of life and followed her star under almost any conditions, however changing. She was of her time and also far ahead of her time. Her mind was open to impressions owing to her early travels and to her study of painting; as an artist she was in sympathy with new ideas and as a young woman she moved in a circle of advanced thought. She had a great affection for things of the past and an encyclopaedic knowledge of the history and details of village domestic life. She was not, however, remotely caught up in a mesh of antiquity-worship.

Unlike many young women of her day she could enter into the feelings of a young Lancashire boy working in a factory and his longing for a garden in a window-box, the only possible kind open to him. *Shirley* had been published in 1849 and *North and South* in 'Household Words' in 1855. This episode of the window box certainly occurred about twenty years later, but, unlike Charlotte Bronte and Mrs Gaskell, Miss Jekyll was living in the heart of the rural south of England and was unacquainted with the conditions of a Rochdale mill or the desolate character of the Yorkshire moors. But still she could picture his 'attic window, under that grey, soot-laden northern sky'.

She welcomed, and indeed introduced, new ideas and among her personal friends were some of the greatest free-thinkers of the time. She had that capacity, strong in William Morris, of making use of her knowledge of the past while striding ahead with ideas for the future. 'We need not reproduce old forms with servility, but if we wish to preserve an English character, we shall look long and carefully at those works which bring down to us the tradition of those who wrought so well for our ancestors.' The writer is Mr Laurence Binyon quoted by Miss Jekyll in her Introduction to *Old English Household Life*. William Morris took many of his designs for the earlier wallpapers from ideas suggested to him by the drawings in Gerard's *Herbal* (1633), which he studied as a young man. But, 'dependent as his work seemed upon the past, he seemed also to begin everything anew, from poetry to woodcuts, from church-windows to wallpapers'.[1]

Ruskin, William Robinson, Madame Bodichon—these were names connected with revolutionary ideas in painting and social conditions, gardening and education, and many of their ideas were shared by Miss Jekyll.

In her own words: 'Sympathetic modern design, imaginative, of good workmanship and making skilful use of local materials, is in every case better than the reproduction of an ancient example, how admirable so-ever.'[2] A summing up of her work and ideas forms the nucleus of an article she wrote about four years before she died. It came out in the *Nineteenth Century*, August, 1928, entitled, 'Changes of Fashion in Gardening'. In it she gives a resumé of the last seventy years of gardening, beginning, of course, with the formal bedding out of half-hardy plants. 'In the greater number of gardens there would be circles and

[1] *William Morris*, by Alfred Noyes.
[2] *Garden Ornament*. Prologue, revised edition, 1927.

stars and crescents, sprinkled about without any sense of design or cohesion. . . . One of the worst and most popular features was what was called a ribbon border—a stiff edging of deep and exactly formed undulations, planted with lines of blue, yellow and scarlet.'

Then she describes the changes—'. . . in the early seventies there came a kind of awakening . . .'—giving credit to a number of amateurs, each discovering and working and encouraging a better perception. There was Mr Peter Barr, whose travels in Spain and Portugal brought varieties of daffodil which until then had only been known in botanical collections. Mr G. F. Wilson was collecting 'all the known lilies of the world', Lord Penzance was working on sweetbriars, the Rev. Reynolds Hole on roses, and the Rev. C. Wolley Dod and Canon Ellacombe 'were growers of a wide range of garden plants and gave willing and most precious help to the many. . . needing better knowledge . . .'. Over and above all these was Mr William Robinson 'to whose vigorous championship of hardy plants, and constant reiteration about the better ways of using them, the beauties and delights of our modern gardens are mainly due'.

The discoveries of men such as Reginald Farrer and Kingdon-Ward, David Douglas and George Forrest, E. H. Wilson and Robert Fortune, were opening up new possibilities in shrubs and roses, bulbs and rock plants, providing a greater stimulus to the flower trade and encouraging more enterprise and interest in flower shows.

Miss Jekyll writes in this article about the development of rock gardens; water gardens; the use of garden ornaments, steps and pavements; wild gardens; shrub gardens and alpine gardens. She mentions the phase of the 'pergola' and its misuse by people who had travelled to Italy and seen the age-long method of training vines. 'The client would say to the designer: "I must have a pergola".' A pergola, like anything else, in its proper position could be decorative as well as useful. 'Its purpose is to be a covered way leading distinctly from one part of the garden to something definite at the end—a summer-house . . . or a built garden house.'

She champions again the use of half-hardy flowers in the flower border, used rightly, and not as in the bedding-out system of fifty years earlier. 'It should be remembered that it was not the fault of the plants themselves that they were unfairly used. . . . But we have now learnt to use them not in garish contrasts, as of old, but in harmonies and concords.' She concluded: '. . . our gardens are becoming more and more enriched by the remarkable discoveries of botanical travellers in the uplands and mountain ranges of Eastern Asia. The amount of material for garden use is now almost bewildering in its abundance. It is for us to employ it worthily; to study the plants and their needs, and at the same time to cultivate a keen sympathy with all that is most beautiful and instructive in Nature; above all, to work with unending patience and unending fervour.'[1]

Miss Jekyll has been described as the first horticultural Impressionist, translating gardening into terms of painting. But she was not only a gardener in colour if the word colour indicates brightness. She understood, as an artist, the use of light and shade. She thought of green as a colour, and repeated often and again the fact that a flower border could not be in full bloom all the time but that periods of green were not only restful but attractive.

She planned her garden planting as she had planned the paints on her canvas. For her gardening was not 'a craft or a science', it was an art.

In 1934 her memorial, designed by Sir Edwin Lutyens, was erected in Busbridge churchyard. The inscription reads:

Artist

Gardener

Craftswoman

The order is significant. It seems to imply that the second and third qualifications depend on the first. More important is her permanent memorial in the ideas and designs which she has passed on to all future generations.

Her work is known and appreciated today in America, in Scandinavia and on the Continent, and her influence may be seen in the work of other contemporary gardeners, especially in those of Brazil. In England it is noticeable how frequently her name appears in current gardening literature—in articles for the *Gardener's Chronicle*, the *Royal Horticultural Society's Journal*, etc. In *Garden Design*, written by Sylvia Crowe, a former President of the Institute of Landscape Architects of England, there is frequent reference to her work. Two of her books have special mention—*Wood and Garden* and *Wall and Water Gardens*, and *Colour in the Flower Garden* appears in the bibliography. There are more references under her name in the index than to anyone else, contemporary or otherwise. This applies also in *The Education of a Gardener* by Russell Page, published by Collins in 1962. The book that he especially mentions is *Wall and Water Gardens*. Her work has also been quoted in wireless programmes and, in a discussion in the programme 'Gardeners' Question Time', she was referred to as an authority on moving well-grown trees and shrubs.

[1] *The Nineteenth Century and After*, July–December, 1928. Constable.

But what about the gardens? Where is there now a Jekyll garden that can be studied, so that her suggestions may be seen when put into practice? It is difficult to keep a garden as it has been kept by someone else. However much one tries to copy ideas, small personal differences will creep in which give an individual character. Perhaps it is more the *atmosphere* of a garden that one should look for, with examples of identical plantings, rather than an exact reproduction of an original. But, as Mr Hussey reminds us: 'She designed the gardens for the majority of the houses built or enlarged by Lutyens in the 'nineties (as she continued to do for thirty years).'[1] And so it is fairly safe to say that any Lutyens house will show some influence of hers in its garden, if it has been kept up as a garden at all. Russell Page goes even farther. He writes: 'I can think of few English gardens made in the last fifty years which do not bear the mark of her teaching, whether in the arrangement of a flower border, the almost habitual association of certain plants or the planting of that difficult passage where garden merges into wild.'[2]

Her own garden at Munstead Wood is well cared for now—it has many of the same features, and the grass paths still lead through the woodland. Round the house her Cape lilies are flourishing. The garden of Millmead is kept well—the small summerhouse built by Lutyens is well established now and has an air of antiquity about it. But however well cared for, it is difficult to see these two without missing her personal touch. At Munstead Wood one special personal touch missing was not a garden one—there was not a cat to be seen.

Some other gardens, quite different in size and type, are still much as they were originally designed, but, again, there are alterations through change in ownership. The first, Hestercombe, now belongs to the Somerset Fire Brigade, who are doing their best to keep the extensive gardens and terraces under the difficulties of a small amount of gardening help. Another is that of 100, Cheyne Walk, originally belonging to Sir Hugh Lane. The house is now converted into flats, but the main structure of the Lutyens garden is the same—the mulberry tree is just a few years older. Miss Jekyll especially mentions this as a typical design suitable for a London garden. An interesting changeover is that of Nashdom, near Taplow, built by Lutyens for Princess Alex Dolgorouki as a fabulous villa for week-end river parties. It is now Nashdom Abbey, the home of twenty-seven Benedictine monks. (1909 was the date of Miss Jekyll's designs for Nashdom.)

And so let us turn to gardens showing her influence or illustrating

[1] *Life of Sir Edwin Lutyens.*　　[2] *The Education of a Gardener.* Collins, 1962.

her ideas either intentionally or quite independently. In some of these examples her influence has been direct—in others there are ideas of which she would have approved. For instance, there is a suggestion of hers which is illustrated at the Waterperry Horticultural School, Wheatley, Oxford. 'The michaelmas daisies are so important in September and October that it is well worth while to give them a separate place, in addition to their use with other flowers in the mixed border.'[1]

In the Savill Gardens there are instances of her suggestions of sending a climbing rose or clematis up into an old fruit tree or a holly. Some of these are also to be seen in the gardens of Sissinghurst Castle. In the garden that Mr and Mrs Lanning Roper created in Onslow Square there are many plantings of her favourite bergenia (megasea) and hostas and there are bushes of Madame Pierre Oger flowering radiantly among the foliage of shrubs and herbaceous plants. At Wisley there are groups of lilies shining in their whiteness between the dark-leaved rhododendrons.[2]

At Folly Farm, Sulhampstead, Berkshire, there are borders of her much-loved grey plants—sprawling shrubs of lavender, senecio, iris foliage, and a fine clump of acanthus. At Spetchley Park, near Droitwich, where Major Berkeley has some of the treasures from Miss Willmott's garden at Warley, there are fine clumps of *Agapanthus intermedius* growing in the border. Miss Jekyll often speaks of growing agapanthus in this way, though she also mentions its possibilities as a tub plant. 'The colour now passes to purpler tones, first the light bluish purple of the dwarf agapanthus, *A. mooreanus*, and its white variety, then by the *eryngiums*—steel blue and silvery white.'[3]

At Bodnant there are slabs of stone used as a border paving between the grass and the edge of the flower beds. At Great Dixter, Northiam, Sussex, there is a strong Jekyll feeling about the garden, giving ample evidence of Mrs Nathaniel Lloyd's appreciation of her ideas, and continued by Mr Christopher Lloyd; grey-leafed plants, lavender, mulleins, and the atmosphere of 'sweet solace' and quiet obtained, perhaps, largely by the leading of one part of the garden into another so that now there is a spacious view and now a secluded arbour with a seat where one may rest. Clumps of meconopsis flourish at Great Dixter, the credit for which Mrs Lloyd gives to Miss Jekyll. On a visit to Munstead, her son had asked Miss Jekyll how she contrived

---

[1] *Colour Planning of the Garden*, by G. F. Tilney, T. Humphreys and W. Irving. Introduction by Miss Jekyll.
[2] *Colour Scheme for the Flower Garden*, p. 14. *Wood and Garden*, p. 37. *House and Garden*, p. 84.
[3] *Country Life*, 18th October, 1924.

to produce such grand clumps. ' "Why are your meconopsis as big as cabbages." "Ah!" Miss Jekyll replied, delighted with the question, "I insist that they are watered twice a day." '

The foregoing are a small selection of gardens where various separate ideas from Miss Jekyll's gardening may be found. There are others, too, in each of the gardens mentioned, especially at Wisley and at the Savill Gardens. At Wisley she had helped to work on the rock garden in its early days when it was the private garden of Mr G. F. Wilson and she particularly admired and envied the planting there of *Primula denticulata* which she tried to emulate at Munstead, without quite the same success. '. . . still I have treasured that lesson among many others I have brought away from that good garden. . . .'[1] In *Wall and Water Garden* she included an illustration of *Gunnera manicata* at Wisley (R.H.S.) (Plate 56). At the Savill Gardens there are magnificent examples of clematis rampaging up into tall trees. All these gardens are open to the public, some of them daily and others at specified times. At Nymans, a garden she is known to have visited, the spring border in the walled garden shows the influence of her planting.

But there is one garden which is probably the best and most complete Jekyll garden still surviving almost in its original planting. It includes many of the individual ideas mentioned above, showing them off to perfection as she originally planted them. (A chapter is devoted to it in *Small Country Houses*.) This garden, open to the public for the benefit of the Queen's Institute of District Nursing through the courtesy of the present owners, Colonel and Mrs S. D. H. Pollen, is Deanery Garden, Sonning, Berkshire—Lutyens and Miss Jekyll worked on it together to the commission of Mr Edward Hudson, editor of *Country Life*. 'House and garden are a single interpenetrating conception—parts roofed over, others open to the sun, with the garden walks leading right into and about the house, and the windows placed to catch the sparkle of a pool or complete the pattern of a terrace. . . . Miss Jekyll's naturalistic planting wedded Lutyens's geometry in a balanced union of both principles (form and natural).'[2]

Miss Jekyll's favourite yellow Banksian rose has survived the winters and climbed up the south front of the house. Lavender hedges, fruit trees with roses growing up through their branches, clumps of mullein standing like sentinels near the top of the circular steps which lead from one level to another—and a wonderful rampaging growth of *Solanum jasminoides* up an east wall, are all evidence of Miss Jekyll's planting.

There is, also, about the garden rather a cloistered air. The paved

[1] *Wood and Garden*, pp. 184–5.   [2] *The Life of Sir Edwin Lutyens*.

courtyard, a high soft-coloured brick wall, terraced levels, with a view looking south towards the church, all give an atmosphere of quiet and dignity and peace. It is an example showing the importance of the love for a garden quite apart from the work that goes into it. It has been greatly loved and cared for, first in the planting and design years ago by Gertrude Jekyll, and afterwards by its owners, and the result is in the atmosphere almost as much as in its obvious beauty.

'An English garden has to be lived in all the year round; so to touch the aesthetic sense it must, like a house, embrace something deeper than a fine collection or an architectural feat.'[1] Miss Jekyll's garden designs had 'this something deeper'. Describing one of 'the most beautiful gardens I have ever seen', Miss Jekyll gives a reason for the beauty, that 'the mind of the owner was so entirely in sympathy with the place. . . .'.[2] This feeling for the garden is something which can best be found in her books, and it derives, of course, from her attitude to life and to her religious belief. There is her store of knowledge, her fund of wisdom. Details of plantings, often accompanied by plans, and always by photographs, are there in abundance to suit any site, size or soil of garden. But, perhaps, in trying to follow her ideas it would be wise to recall the kind of person that she was, and the philosophy that lay behind her work; the regard for nature, the reverence for detail, the appreciation of the veining in a small leaf just as much as for a fine lily, the persistence and respect for work, the faith and trust in the ordering of life.

'And a garden is a grand teacher. It teaches patience and careful watchfulness; it teaches industry and thrift; above all, it teaches entire trust. "Paul planteth and Apollos watereth, but God giveth the increase." The good gardener knows with absolute certainty that if he does his part, if he gives the labour, the love, and every aid that his knowledge of craft, experience of the conditions of his place, and exercise of his personal wit can work together to suggest, that so surely as he does this diligently and faithfully, so surely will God give the increase.'[3]

'It must have been at about seven years of age that I first learnt to know and love a primrose copse. Since then more than half a century has passed, and yet each spring, when I wander into the primrose wood, and see the pale yellow blooms, and smell their sweetest scents, and feel the warm spring air throbbing with the quickening pulse of new life,

[1] *Guide to Nymans*, by the Countess of Rosse.   [2] *Wood and Garden*, p. 175.
[3] Ibid., Introduction.

and hear the glad notes of the birds and the burden of the bees, and see again the same delicate young growths piercing the mossy woodland carpet; when I see and feel and hear all this, for a moment I am seven years old again and wandering in the fragrant wood hand-in-hand with the dear God who made it, and who made the child's mind to open wide and receive the enduring happiness of the gracious gift. So, as by direct divine teaching the impression of the simple sweetness of the primrose wood sank deep into the childish heart, and laid, as it were, a foundation stone of immutable belief, that a Father in Heaven who could make all this, could make even better if He would, when the time should come that His children should be gathered about Him.

'And as the quick years pass and the body grows old around the still young heart, and the day of death grows ever nearer; with each new springtide the sweet flowers come forth and bloom afresh; and with their coming—with the ever renewing of their gracious gift and still more precious promise—the thought of death becomes like that of a gentle and kindly bearer of tidings, who brings the inevitable message, and bids the one for whom it is destined receive it manfully and be of good hope and cheerfulness, and remember that the Sender of Death is the Giver of the greater new Life, no less than of the sweet spring flowers, that bloom and die and live again as a never-ending parable of Life and Death and Immortality.'[1]

[1] 'Epilogue', by Gertrude Jekyll from *A Gardener's Testament*. Country Life, 1937.

Bibliography

WORKS BY GERTRUDE JEKYLL

(*The editions used in the preparation of this book are given in parenthesis*)

Wood and Garden. Longmans, Green. 1899.

Home and Garden. Longmans, Green. 1900.

Lilies for English Gardens. Country Life. 1901 (1903).

Wall and Water Gardens. Country Life. 1901 (1913).

Roses for English Gardens (with Edward Mawley). Country Life. 1902.

Old West Surrey. Longmans, Green. 1904.

Some English Gardens (After Drawings by George S. Elgood, R.I.). Longmans, Green, 1904 (4th edition 1906).

Flower Decoration in the House. Country Life. 1907.

Colour in the Flower Garden. Country Life. 1908 (3rd edition 1914 entitled *Colour Schemes for the Flower Garden*).

Children and Gardens. Country Life. 1908 (1933).

Gardens for Small Country Houses (with Lawrence Weaver). Country Life. 1912 (6th edition 1927).

Garden Ornament (with Christopher Hussey). Country Life. 1918 (2nd edition 1927).

Old English Household Life. B. T. Batsford. 1925.

A Gardener's Testament. Country Life. 1937.

WORKS RELATING TO GERTRUDE JEKYLL

Architecture and Personalities. Herbert Baker. Country Life. 1944.

The Barber's Clock. E. V. Lucas. Methuen. 1931.

A Blessed Girl. Lady Emily Lutyens. Rupert Hart-Davis. 1953.

Bricks and Flowers. Memoirs of Katherine Everett: Constable. 1949.

Rajah Brooke and Baroness Burdett-Coutts. Owen Rutter (Ed.). Hutchinson. 1935.

The Coming of Flowers. A. W. Anderson. Williams and Norgate. 1950.

The Curious Gardener. Jason Hill. Faber and Faber. 1932.

Curtis's Botanical Magazine Dedications 1827-1927. Ernest Nelmes and William Cuthbertson, V.M.H. (Comps.). Bernard Quaritch. 1931.

Letters From Charles Dickens to Angela Burdett-Coutts, 1841-1865. Edgar Johnson (Ed.). Jonathan Cape. 1953.

The Education of a Gardener. Russell Page. Collins. 1962.

The English Flower Garden. William Robinson. John Murray. 1897 (5th Edition), 1956 (16th Edition).

The English Garden. Ralph Dutton. B. T. Batsford. 1937.

English Leaves. E. V. Lucas. Methuen. 1933.

English Social History. G. M. Trevelyan. Longmans, Green. 1944.

Even more for your Garden. V. Sackville West. Michael Joseph. 1958.

Flowers and Their Histories. Alice M. Coats. Hulton Press. 1956.

Garden Design. Sylvia Crowe. Country Life.

The Garden of Today. H. Avray Tipping. Martin Hopkinson. 1933.

A Garden in Venice. F. Eden. Country Life. 1903.

Gardenage, or the Plants of Ninhursaga. Geoffrey Grigson. Routledge and Kegan Paul. 1952.

Gardens of Delight. Eleanour Sinclair Rohde. The Medici Society. 1934.

Gardens in the Modern Landscape. Christopher Tunnard. Architectural Press. 1948.

Girton College, 1869-1932. Barbara Stephen. Cambridge University Press. 1933.

The Glass of Fashion. Cecil Beaton. Weidenfeld and Nicolson. 1954.

Gone Rustic. Cecil Roberts. Hodder and Stoughton. 1934.

Great Morning. Osbert Sitwell. Macmillan. 1948.

Octavia Hill. William Thomson Hill. Hutchinson. 1956.

Gertrude Jekyll. Francis Jekyll. Jonathan Cape. 1934.

The Life of Sir Edward Lutyens. Christopher Hussey. Country Life. 1953.

The Life Story of H.R.H. Princess Louise, Duchess of Argyll. David Duff. Stanley Paul. 1940.

On the Making of Gardens. George Sitwell. Gerald Duckworth. 1951 (3rd Edition).

Marianne Thornton. E. M. Forster. Edward Arnold. 1956.

Modern Painting. George Moore. Walter Scott. 1898.

William Morris of Walthamstow. H. V. Wiles. The Walthamstow Press. 1951.

William Nicholson. Lillian Browse. Rupert Hart-Davis. 1956.

William Nicholson. Marguerite Steen. Collins. 1943.

Florence Nightingale 1820-1910. Cecil Woodham-Smith. Constable. 1950.

The Life of Florence Nightingale. Sir Edward Cook. Macmillan. 1925.

The Nineteenth Century, and After. Vol. 104, Nos. 19-20, 1928 (July-Dec.) Constable.

The Order of Release—the story of John Ruskin, Effie Gray, and John Everett Millais. Sir William James (Ed.). John Murray. 1948.

Our River. George D. Leslie. Bradbury, Agnew. 1888.

The Works of Sir Joseph Paxton, 1803-1865. George F. Chadwick. The Architectural Press. 1961.

Pioneers in Gardening. Miles Hadfield. Routledge and Kegan Paul. 1955.

Pilgrimage for Plants. Frank Kingdon-Ward. George G. Harrap. 1960.

Pot-Pourri from a Surrey Garden. Mrs C. W. Earle. Smith, Elder. 1898.

More Pot-Pourri. Mrs. C. W. Earle. Smith, Elder. 1898.

Retrospect of Flowers. Andrew Young. Jonathan Cape. 1950.

Reperusals and Recollections. Logan Pearsall Smith. Constable. 1937.

A Book About Roses. S. Reynolds Hole. Edward Arnold. 1891. (11th Edition.)

John Ruskin. Frederic Harrison. Macmillan. 1902.

Sir Edwin Lutyens: An Appreciation in Perspective. Robert Lutyens. Country Life.

The Life of John Ruskin. E. T. Cook (Vols 1 and 2). George Allen. 1911.

The Scarlet Tree. Osbert Sitwell. Macmillan. 1945-50.

The Scented Garden. Eleanour Sinclair Rohde. The Medici Society. 1957.

The Schools of Design. Quentin Bell. Routledge and Kegan Paul. 1963.

The Stranger's Companion in Chester. G. Batenham (5th Edition).

Travels and Discoveries in the Levant (Vols 1 and 2). C. T. Newton. Day and Son. 1865.

The Victorian Flower Garden. Geoffrey Taylor. Skeffington. 1952.

The Letters of Lord and Lady Wolseley, 1870-1911. Sir George Arthur (Ed.) William Heinemann. 1922.

In Your Garden. V. Sackville-West. Michael Joseph. 1951.

Index

INDEX OF FLOWERS, PLANTS, SHRUBS, &c.